C1

978
HIL

Hill, William E.

The Oregon Trail,
yesterday and
today

DATE DUE

FEB 0 4 1995	
MAY 1 0 1995	
APR 0 9 1996	
SEP 1 4 1998	
JUL 3 0 2001	
JUL 3 0 2001	
MAY 0 8 2002	
MAY 3 1 2005	

GAYLORD   PRINTED IN U.S.A.

© THE BAKER & TAYLOR CO.

Key to Site Locations on the Oregon Trail

1 — Westport Landing
2 — Independence Square
3 — Shawnee Methodist Mission
4 — St. Marys Mission
5 — Alcove Spring
6 — Hollenberg Ranch
7 — Rock Creek Station
8 — Fort Kearny
9 — Ash Hollow
10 — Courthouse and Jail Rock
11 — Jackson Panorama — Platte River
12 — Chimney Rock
13 — Castle Rock
14 — Scotts Bluff and Mitchell Pass
15 — Fort Laramie
16 — Register Cliff and Oregon Trail Ruts
17 — Laramie Peak
18 — Fort Caspar
19 — Red Buttes — Bessemer Bend
20 — Rock Avenue and Willow Springs Area
21 — Independence Rock
22 — Devil's Gate Area
23 — Split Rock
24 — Three Crossings

25 — St. Mary's Station
26 — Rocky Ridge
27 — Burnt Ranch
28 — Twin Mounds
29 — South Pass Area and Dry Sandy Crossing
30 — Haystack Butte
31 — Case Ferry
32 — Fort Bridger
33 — Bear Mountain Descent
34 — Fort Hall
35 — Three Island Crossing
36 — Snake River Bluffs
37 — Lizard Butte
38 — Fort Boise
39 — Keeney Pass
40 — Farewell Bend
41 — Ladd Canyon and Grande Ronde
42 — Blue Mountains
43 — Descent of Blue Mountains
44 — Whitman Mission
45 — The Dalles
46 — Barlow Road and Mt. Hood
47 — Oregon City
48 — Fort Vancouver

OREGON TRAIL

BRANCHES OR ALTERNATE ROUTES

THE OREGON TRAIL:
Yesterday and Today

A Brief History and Pictorial Journey
Along the Wagon Tracks of Pioneers

by

WILLIAM E. HILL

The CAXTON PRINTERS, Ltd.
Caldwell, Idaho
1987

Library of Congress Cataloging-in-Publication Data

Hill, William E.
  The Oregon Trail, yesterday and today.

    Bibliography: p.
    Includes index.
    1. Oregon Trail. 2. Overland journeys to the
Pacific. 3. West (U.S.) — History. 4. West (U.S.) —
Description and travel — 1981-   — Guide-books.
I. Title.
F597.H65   1987   978   86-6134
ISBN 0-87004-319-6 (pbk.)

Printed and bound in the United States of America by
The Caxton Printers, Ltd.
Caldwell, Idaho 83605
143981

C 1

TO HELEN, AND IN MEMORY OF PAUL

Contents

Illustrations

Maps

The Oregon Trail

THE OREGON TRAIL started at Independence, Missouri and continued for approximately two thousand miles until it reached Oregon City on the Willamette River. It would head west across the prairies of Kansas, northwest along the Little Blue into Nebraska, west through the Platte River Valley, and along the North Platte, crossing over to the Sweetwater River to the great South Pass, and then on across the valley of the Green River to the valley of the Bear River; up the Bear, crossing to the Snake River, along the Snake, and finally leaving to cut over to the Columbia River, on to The Dalles, and at last to the valley of the Willamette and Oregon City. Traveling about twenty miles a day, the journey would take most emigrants four and one-half to five months. Many would die trying, while others would turn around. That most made it is a credit to the human will and spirit. . . .

Preface

A S ONE INTERESTED in history and wanting better to understand the past, I became drawn to visiting the places where history was made. I hoped that in some small or perhaps gigantic way, I would understand better what it was really like back in "those days," and perhaps even have the same feelings as the people involved in the historical events that happened in those locations.

This interest in historical places was in no small part due to my yearly summer vacation trips taken by my family to historical sites and national parks when I was young. After establishing a family of my own, the desire to visit them continued. For the past twelve years, my family and I have been sightseeing along the Oregon Trail, reading diaries and guide books, and then trying to locate the very same spots where earlier pioneers had experienced and recorded specific events. I had hoped to find the exact areas and natural settings, so as to enrich my personal knowledge of the trek westward that so many emigrants had taken. I became interested also in early drawings and photographs depicting the journey and hoped to locate the same spots that the frontier artists had used.

However, over the years I have noticed various forces at work which made difficult both experiencing the trail in its natural setting and finding the specific locations. Civilization and time had marched on since the days when the early Oregon emigrants had traveled across the plains. But that was too general a statement or explanation for the changes that have occurred. Each year that I returned, it seemed to grow increasingly difficult, since more of the trail had disappeared.

There seemed to be three major factors responsible for this. First was our expansion and changes in the agricultural use of the land. This was due to land-leveling and the wider use of irrigation with the need to control water and rivers. Second and more recent was the growing oil shortage, which resulted in wider exploration and construction of wells, pipelines, and other developments which necessitated additional traffic in many areas of the Oregon Trail. Both these factors have led to the destruction of trail ruts in numerous places from central Nebraska to Oregon. However, the most unfortunate occurrence has been the vandalism by other travelers and souvenir hunters. Some locations have been vandalized so much that owners do not encourage or even allow visitors to enter. The Wyoming Historical Society and the Bureau of Land Management had placed concrete markers with bronze medallions along the trail in many areas. Yet so many of these markers have been broken or stolen that newer ones had to be made, but without the bronze medallions. And, it seems that even these can't be replaced fast enough to keep up with the desecrators. Grave markers and the different register rocks have had to be fenced to keep them from being further defaced. Some displays are scratched and broken, and even the stone placed by Paul Henderson and L. C. Bishop at the "Parting of the Ways" has been taken.

One additional change along the area of the trail has been the growth of trees. Shortly after leaving Independence, the early emigrants entered the treeless plains — a sea of rolling prairie grasses. For most of the journey trees were a rare sight and frequently the few that existed were soon cut down for firewood. This was the case with the famous Lone Elm out on the Kansas plains and the Lone Pine in Oregon which became some emigrant's campfire. Emigrants were forced to rely on "buffalo chips" and sage for firewood. As the emigrants moved west and settled, the prairies were plowed, and trees were planted and spread. Today, many sights are now obscured by trees. The Blue Mound in Kansas and much of the valley of the Platte River are now in trees, and thus gives the traveler of today a false impression.

However, on the brighter side, a number of positive steps have been taken to help us hold onto what is left of the Oregon Trail. The federal government through the National Park Service has had the Oregon Trail designated as a National Historic Trail. The National Park Service has identified one hundred twenty-five sites of historical significance which they are trying to save. They are also attempting to establish seven cross-country hiking segments in areas where the trail is still pristine or has a natural appearance. Wyoming has two of the segments, including the longest one. Idaho has two and Oregon three. Living museums have been set up at a number of the historic sites by the National Park Service, and even the states and historical societies have encouraged the development of displays and living museums in the areas they control.

One of the largest and best is at Fort Laramie in Wyoming under the management of the National Park Service, and one of the newest is a small one still developing at Rock Creek, Nebraska, under the state game and parks commission. But if you were to talk to Wayne Brandt, the superintendent, it would sound like it will be one of the greatest. It is that interest and spirit that has been re-kindled that will save the trail. Among others, the highway departments seem to have felt the resurgence in interest. Many of the highway rest areas have set up appropriate displays and are worth exploring. Since most of the trail is owned by private citizens, it will be up to them to help preserve parts. While some shy away from having visitors or specifically prohibit trespassing, many will go out of their way to tell you what they know about the trail or local history, and are trying to preserve it. Most recently has been the formation of the

Oregon-California Trail Association dedicated to preserving the remnants of the trail and the historic sites along it.

This book is designed to give only a brief introduction to the Oregon Trail experience and its history. Many other books have been written which cover the subject in more detail, but this is for the beginner. It was the type of book I longed for when I started my travels over the trail. It is hoped that it will arouse your interest.

Recent publications by Aubrey Haines — *Historic Sites Along the Oregon Trail* — and Gregory Franzwa's *Oregon Trail Revisited* and *Maps of the Oregon Trail* are a boon to any person interested in trail travel today. It must be noted that these were built on the works of Paul and Helen Henderson, who for years traveled and mapped the Oregon Trail. For further and more detailed information about the trail and its history, a short list of books is included in the bibliography which should be both helpful and interesting for those willing to read more.

WILLIAM E. HILL
Centereach, New York
1987

Introduction

Misconceptions and Realities

LIKE MOST PEOPLE brought up in the age of T.V., we all have developed many ideas about the trek west and the Oregon Trail. Unfortunately, Hollywood has not always strived for historical accuracy when making movies about them. Talk to any child and you will readily see that many misconceptions and "myths" have resulted.

One is the concept of the trail, or the route itself. It seems that people either see the trail as one road that never changed, or more likely as some vague route on which a solitary wagon or perhaps a wagon train traveled alone, breaking new ground and never knowing exactly where they were.

The reality of the trail is that it was more like a braided band, frayed at the ends, which meandered a little with each year and with changing weather conditions. While in certain locations such as Robidoux's Pass, or later at Michell Pass, the trail did converge into a single passage, in other places the wagon trains might have spread out up to one-half mile wide or more. In places, there were many parallel routes, sometimes a few miles away from each other. Emigrants tried frequent "shortcuts," hoping to save time on their westward journey. At times these shortcuts proved to be successful and at other times they were disastrous.

Most of the emigrants did not journey out onto the prairies alone, but joined a wagon company often comprised of family, relatives, friends, or people from the same area. The very early emigrants usually hired a trapper to pilot them, but after the mid-to-late 1840s, there was less need for a pilot, and most did not hire one. Except for the first few years, even wagon companies were not alone, but usually within sight of one company or another. This was especially true during the first half of the journey and even further west, companies were usually only hours or at most a day away. By sampling of diaries and reports at Fort Kearny and Fort Laramie for different years, one can see the crowded nature of the trail. At Fort Kearny, three hundred twenty miles out on the trail five hundred wagons were reported to have rolled by in one day during the peak year of 1849. On May 26, 1850, James Evans estimated that about two thousand emigrants were encamped near the fort. Reports concerning the fort's ledger showed that by June 5, 1852, some twenty thousand men and four thousand women had passed this place. For Fort Laramie, which was situated six hundred fifty miles out on the trail, John Unruh notes that from the reconstructed register of 1850, two thousand eighteen people and five hundred fifty wagons went through on June 6, and on June 17, the peak day, six thousand thirty-four people were on the road.

Clearly, most emigrants were not alone. James Wilkins wrote on June 13, while traveling between the forks of the Platte River:

"Find a great many companies continually in sight. In fact it is one continued stream. As far as we can see, both in front and near the horizon is dotted with white wagon covers of emigrants, like a string of beads." Diaries frequently mentioned meeting and passing other wagon companies and competing with them for forage in the evenings. Other diaries mentioned how wagon companies split up and parts joined other companies throughout their trek. Below is a list of successful Oregon-bound emigrants taken from Unruh's *The Plains Across* (University of Illinois Press). Also listed are the California-Utah emigrants. Other historians may have different figures.

Emigration by Year and Destination

Year	Oregon	Utah and California
1840	13	0
1841	24	34
1842	125	0
1843	875	38
1844	1,475	53
1845	2,500	260
1846	1,200	1,500
1847	4,000	2,650
1848	1,300	2,800
1849	450	26,500
1850	6,000	46,500
1851	3,600	2,600
1852	10,000	60,000
1853	7,500	28,000
1854	6,000	15,167
1855	500	6,184
1856	1,000	10,200
1857	1,500	5,300
1858	1,500	6,150
1859	2,000	18,431

(Note the year 1849 as it shows the impact of the California Gold Rush and the years just prior to that shows the beginning of the Mormon migrations to Utah.)

While it seems that most traveled together by choice, there were a number of other reasons for the different wagon companies to become "bunched," even if they wished not to do so. These reasons were primarly due to the climatic and terrain conditions of the plains. The first was related to the need for grass and forage to feed their stock along the trail. Wagon companies could not realistically leave their jumping-off places until the springtime when the grasses were out. A second was the necessity for getting over the Blue and

Cascade Mountains in Oregon before the snows. These caused most companies to leave late in April and May. Leaving in June could cause one to be caught in the snows in the mountains or finding it hard to obtain grass in the immediate vicinity of the trail.

Some of the late departing companies would leave the trail for three miles or more to find forage in the evenings. If one left earlier than April, there would be no grass for the stock. A third factor was the violent and unpredictable prairie storms which could cause rivers and streams to flood and back up companies at river crossings for days. In 1843 Pierson Readings noted that the Kansas River was full and "swimming with very rapid current." William Newby in the same company wrote, "We reacht the Caw River the 25 of May . . . We had some difficulty in crawsing. The bote sunck with one family, tho all waws save. We made a bote & had all over in 6 days." Two years later when Jacob Synder was there, their company crossed it in only one day. As a result of all these factors, most companies traveled in the "company" or close proximity of other wagon companies.

Within a few years after the migration west started, travel guidebooks became available to the emigrants. While some were better that others, they often included information about mileage references, locations for major stream and river crossings, spring sites, availability of grass, comments about the nature of the road, and major sights or attractions. One of the earliest and more popular ones was Landsford Hastings' *The Emigrant's Guide to Oregon and California — 1845*. For the Mormons, there was the excellent book by William Clayton, *The Latter Day Saints' Emigrant's Guide* which covered the first half of the trail to Oregon. Others continued to come out during this period. Johnson & Winter, Palmer, Shively, Ware, Child, Horn, and Marcy all had guidebooks of varying quality.

For the companies leaving shortly after the first trains, and especially during the years of heavy traffic, the trail itself

became a well-marked and beaten path. Father DeSmet in
1851 described the trail in the Platte Valley as "this noble
highway which is as smooth as a barn floor swept by the
winds, and not a blade of grass can shoot up on it account
of continued passing." In a manner of speaking, it seems,
once you were in the rut, you stayed there all the way. In
many places today, the wagon trail and ruts are still visible
for the traveler to follow. Sometimes they are about one
hundred feet wide and in others, only one swale wide. All
this, however, is not to say that wagons did not get lost or
caught in the snows, or both. Perhaps the most famous of
these unfortunates was the Donner Party of 1846–7 on its
way to California along a new, unproved route.

Travelers also had numerous landmarks along the way
which they used as guide posts. Some of the most famous
included: the Blue Mound, Courthouse & Jail Rock, Chimney
Rock, Scott's Bluff, Laramie Peak, Independence Rock and
Devil's Gate, Split Rock, the Wind River Mountains, Twin
Buttes near the South Pass, Three Buttes near Fort Hall, and
later Mount Hood. Many of these are included in this book,
and all served to keep the emigrants heading in the right
direction.

The trail was marked also in more unfortunate ways.
One was by the goods that were often discarded beside the
trail. Sometimes emigrants even left notes on the items telling
others to take what they needed. However, some emigrants
reportedly destroyed what they discarded so those coming
later could not make use of the items left. Only nine days
out on the trail, Israel Hale mentioned frequently seeing
flour, bacon, and other provisions along the route, and later
notes seeing from one-to-three cast iron stoves everyday for
nearly two weeks. Another emigrant wrote, "Along the banks
of the North Platte to where the Sweetwater road turns off,
the amount of valuable property thrown away is astonishing
— iron, trunks, clothing, &c., lying strewed about to the
value of at least fifty thousand dollars in about twenty miles."

And between Fort Laramie and the Green River, "I have counted one thousand wagons that have been burnt or otherwise disposed of on the road." While the thousand-wagon figure seems high, the value of the goods is more believable.

Death was another "marker" on the trail. Along the drier and harsher segments of the trail, carcasses of dead animals marked the area. J. Goldsborough Bruff wrote on July 27, 1849, "Dead cattle marking the trail, as usual." And in the very bad years of cholera, graves would show the route. Cecelia Adams noted that on June 18, 1852, there were twenty-one newly-made graves while traveling only eighteen miles that day. Not all days, however, were that bad.

While all rivers and streams had to be crossed, not all had to be forded. The emigrants were enterprising young people with a capitalistic nature that soon became evident whenever time allowed. Within a few years of trail traffic, some bridges or ferries had been established. Often an emigrant, after making a raft for himself to cross the river, would spend a couple of days ferrying other wagons for a fee. Enoch Conyers did just that after he crossed the Snake River successfully in 1852, and made $33.50 in one day.

Some emigrants chose to stay longer and built permanent bridges and ferries; a few even graded whole roads and charged a fee. Some of the more famous ones were: the Papin Ferry at the Kansas (Kaw) River; Vieux's Bridge at the Red Vermillion; the various ferries and bridges over the North Platte between Deer Creek and the Red Buttes; the Mormon, Mountainmen, Case, and Lombard ferries over the Green River; and the famous Barlow Road over the Cascades. By the early 1850s it seemed that bridges and ferries existed at the major crossings and many of the minor ones. Nevertheless, many emigrants chose to ford the streams instead of using these improvements because they could not afford or did not wish to pay the high tolls. In 1852, fees on the ferries and bridges ranged from twenty-five cents at the Portneuf Creek bridge to sixteen dollars per wagon at the Green River Ferry. It was reported that two entrepreneurs at the Green River Ferry made about sixty-five thousand dollars that same year. The average charge, it seemed, was about three dollars per wagon.

Many movies show the wagon trains full of people riding in big wagons pulled by horses. In reality, most people walked because their wagons held more valuable cargo — the supplies and furnishings needed to establish their new homes in Oregon. Some people did not have wagons at all, and rode horseback. There are even accounts of people riding "cowback" for part of the trail. Others went west with handcarts, animal carts, and even a few rode in carriages. While horses were used by some, mules and oxen were better suited. Their endurance was greater and they were less likely to be stolen by the Indians. And contrary to that which is shown in some movies and displays, the emigrants usually did not use the big heavy Conestoga wagons of the East, but a smaller, lighter wagon more suitable on the westward trek.

While almost every western film shows circled wagon trains being attacked by Indians, this was really a rare occurrence for most emigrants. During the early years of the trail, the emigrants were more likely to encounter the Indians as traders or as some saw them, as beggars or petty thieves looking for horses rather than as a hostile force. Many emigrants noted that they rarely had any encounters with the Indians. This does not mean that they were not wary of them. Most of the later emigrants thought of the Indians as being inferior and treated them as such. Not until the Indian Wars of the 1860s did the natives really cause any long or major disruptions to the traffic west. It is true that most wagon companies circled when nooning or camping in the evening, but this was done more to keep control of their stock than for defense against the Indians. The few times when the Indians did attack, it was usually when the wagons were strung out. John Unruh estimated that only about four percent of all deaths along the trail was due to Indian attacks.

Others might place it lower. The chart below is based on this work.

Deaths Due to Indian Attacks

Year	Number of Deaths	Year	Number of Deaths
1840	0	1850	48
1841	0	1851	60
1842	0	1852	45
1843	0	1853	7
1844	0	1854	35
1845	4	1855	6
1846	4	1856	20
1847	24	1857	17
1848	2	1858	(?)
1849	33	1859	32

Thus, it shows that during the early pre-gold rush years, the emigrants suffered little at the hands of the Indians, except for one train at Tule Lake on the Southern Oregon or Applegate route in 1847. And, in the perspective of history, these deaths caused by all the Indian attacks during the early years of trail travel where far fewer than those caused by automobile accidents in one of our more populous states in a single summer.

A greater threat to the life and limb of the emigrant was due to accidents and disease. These were the real killers of the plains. Most diaries included reports of someone hurt or killed by firearms or animals, accidental drownings, or getting run over by a wagon. During the 1842 emigration, Medorem Crawford recorded the death of the Lancaster baby girl five days out from Independence due to disease. Later, near Independence Rock, a young man named Baily was killed due to an accidental discharge of a gun from a wagon, and the Bennitt's girl was slightly wounded two days later. Crawford mentioned that the young man responsible for the accidental killing was later drowned in a river crossing. In the 1843 migration, one of the earliest deaths recorded on the trail was that of Joel Hembree. William Newby wrote in 1843, "A very bad road. Joel J. Hembree son Joel fel off the waggeon tung & both wheels run over him." Joel was only six years old.

Little was known about health and sanitation, and there were no vaccinations available. Opportunities for bathing and laundering were severely limited. Human and animal wastes, garbage, putrified animal carcasses, and available water supplies were often in close proximity. And, in some parts of the journey, pure drinking water was simply not available in sufficient quantities for all. Even when wagon companies tried to be careful to find safe areas to camp at night, it often proved impossible due to the proximity of other trains and the darkness of the night.

When the Burn's wagon came to the Marsh Creek campground in 1852, they headed upstream to camp for the night and took their water from the creek. While William Burns was walking along the stream, he discovered eight to ten dead cattle and mules lying in and around the creek. He returned very quickly with the information. Immediately the emigrants emptied their kettles and pots. William headed back upstream to get above the dead animals where the water would be safe and returned to camp with "good water." The next morning, Enoch Conyers took the pail to get the water. He found the spot where William had gotten the water, but to his dismay the creek was still littered with dead carcasses. He went more than a half mile further, but the creek bottom was full of dead animals. He returned with no water, and others at the camp had counted fifty carcasses near their wagons. They broke camp and left. These were the reasons that disease could easily take its heavy toll.

As in the case of Indian attacks, certain years were worse than others for deaths due to disease. Cholera, the biggest killer of all diseases, was at its worst during the gold rush years of 1849, 1850, and 1852. Almost every diary makes mention of a death of a member somewhere along the trail, or even before a trek started. Rare was the wagon company that did not experience it. Maj. Moses "Black" Harris, famous mountain man and pilot, died in a bed in Independence, Missouri, just before he was to guide a wagon train west. Israel Hale, writing in 1849, noted that cholera took its first victim on the fifth day out of St. Joseph, Missouri, and that it was only ten hours from the time he took sick until he died and was buried. More deaths were to follow. Estimates for each of the years noted above have been placed at two thousand.

Estimates of emigrant deaths from all causes on the overland trails range from Wisner's thirty thousand to Unruh's ten thousand for the pre-1860 era. Thus, it seems between four percent to six percent of the emigrants died along the way. Or, as other historians have explained it, about one grave for every five hundred feet.

As shown, many of the concepts people have about the trail and travel along it are inaccurate, and the realities are sometimes almost the opposite.

THE OREGON TRAIL:
Yesterday and Today

Part I
Tracks of the Prairie Schooners

Experiences Along the Trail Today

FOR THE SERIOUS traveler of the Oregon Trail, it is still possible to get the feeling of the trek west and even a chance to "see the elephant" that the early emigrants encountered. All that is needed is patience, lots of time, a sturdy vehicle with four-by-four drive, some good luck, and some bad luck. Passenger cars and recreation vehicles are fine for the highway, but not for various segments of the trail. And in some spots, only shoe leather will enable the traveler to make the passage.

Diaries of early emigrants mentioned torrential downpours, flooding of streams and rivers, the dust, hail storms, mosquitos, snakes, muddy roads, breakdowns, oxen with bad feet, having to dig up and down ravines, death of their animals, the heat of the day and cold of the night, and buffalo stampedes. On the brighter side were the different animals, meetings with friendly Indians, the beautiful starry nights, the natural wonders, and the rolling prairies.

Most of these can still be experienced. Gone are the buffalo. Except for some buffalo in parks and zoos along the trail, one has to travel further away to see them roam. But a very lucky person might still find part of a buffalo skull as happened recently to a friend. One animal encountered often was the antelope; today they seem to thrive and may even be in greater numbers than when the emigrants were crossing the plains. This seems to be especially true in Wyoming. As for the Indians, they, too, have been driven from most of the lands they first inhabited. Fortunately, there has been a resurgence of interest in their native culture. By timing your trip right, you can visit nearby reservations and attend some of their celebrations. This may also require a side trip, but it is well worth it.

The rolling prairies are almost gone, covered over with the trappings of civilization and burgeoning population growth, but with a little imagination, there are still a few places where they can be experienced. As one gets further into some of the sections of western Nebraska, Wyoming, Idaho, and Oregon, the trail can still be seen and experienced in its natural setting. The starry nights in the West are still the most beautiful, especially next to your own campfire as was experienced at Ash Hollow and later at Three Island Crossing. In both places, campgrounds are in the same locations that emigrants used. The squinting of your eyes looking for the great landmarks and the excitement and thrill of seeing them — the first sighting of Courthouse Rock, Chimney Rock, Independence Rock, and Devil's Gate, the great Wind River Mountains covered with snow, and Mount Hood — they are all still there just waiting for you to see. The biggest contrast is that for the eager pioneer in his slow-moving wagon, the first sighting could be days away, while for the modern traveler, the distances may be covered in hours, or even a few minutes in some cases.

As for the more unpleasant aspects of trail life and travel, they've all been experienced by the author — fortunately never all in one trip. One year we ran into torrential rains that nearly flooded the bridge over the Wakarusa and did flood the roads, causing delays and detours. The fine powdery dust on Sublette's Flats caused one's eyes to burn and to cough even when the doors and windows were tightly closed. A hail storm near Torrington, Wyoming, made one happy to have a hard top in place of only canvas covering the "wagon" . . . ferocious and hungry mosquitos that attack at Three Crossings near Jeffrey City . . . stepping out of your car to find rattlesnakes east of Independence Rock and later near Farewell Bend . . . getting stuck in the mud on the Slate

Creek Cutoff . . . a car breakdown near St. Mary's Station, and a three-day layover in Jeffrey City to have it fixed after just barely getting back . . . getting stuck in a ravine at Bridger Creek and having to dig my way out, my wife and son having me stop so they could pick up the skulls and other bones from dead cattle and antelope . . . fording the John Day River and numerous little streams . . . blazing a new path where the old trail was washed away . . . praying that the air conditioner would keep working . . . going on a buffalo chase southwest of Laramie when someone had left the gate open on the range where Bison Pete's buffalo still "roam" . . . and last but not least, having gone through both spare tires on Sublette's Flat near Monument Butte, which resulted in my "turnaround." None of these, however, should be seen as obstacles but only as a means of truly getting to experience and know the feeling of the trail as the emigrants themselves might have. For those who truly strive to find it, the trail is still there!

Early History of the Great Trail West

DEVELOPMENT OF THE Oregon Trail, heading into setting sun drew explorers, adventurers, mountain men and pioneers like some giant magnet. It was adventure, romance, excitement, and a chance to start a new life on land of your own. "Go West, young man, and grow up with the country," was the advice given by Horace Greeley, and thousands took up the challenge. "Oregon" was the name on everyone's lips in the years before the California Gold Rush. The manner in which it unfolded is the story of one of the greatest migrations of all time, as sketched below and on subsequent pages, beginning with the purchase of the vast Louisiana Territory which few had ever seen, other than the natives . . .

1803 — President Thomas Jefferson purchased the Louisana Territory from the French. Some people saw this as a gross extension of his power as president, but it did turn America's eyes westward. While this did not give clear title to the area we call Oregon, it provided an additional basis for part of the claim. It gave the U.S. title to the lands that the Oregon Trail crossed. The Oregon area west of the continental divide was contested by the United States, Britain, Spain, and Russia.

1804–6 — Meriwether Lewis and William Clark set out on their expedition to explore the newly-purchased lands. They ventured further than that with the instructions to ". . . explore the Missouri River, and such principal stream of it, as, by it's course and communication with the waters of the Pacific Ocean . . ." They were to map the area, record information about plants, animals, and the native people in the area. They returned with stories of animals — the beaver — and bountiful lands and waters — the Willamette in the Oregon Territory. These were to arouse the dreams of fur trappers and farmers alike, and to strengthen America's claim to the Oregon Territory.

1812–13 — John Jacob Astor decided to compete with the British for the fur trade in the Pacific Northwest. A party of his "Astorians" led by Robert Stuart returned to St. Louis, Missouri, from the Columbia River with tales of their journey and the wealth of furs. Stuart, it seemed, learned of the South Pass, but because of apparent Indian traffic, did not use it. It would be another twelve years before it would be used. In one sense Stuart was the first to complete the Oregon Trail, only in reverse.

1818 — Treaty of 1818 was signed between the United States and Great Britain fixing the northern border at the forty-ninth parallel from Lake of the Woods in Minnesota to the Rocky Mountains. It provided also for the joint occupation of the Oregon Territory, and allowed for the settlement and existence of fur trading companies of both nations. This was renewable in ten years, and it was so renewed.

1819 — Adams-Onis Treaty was signed between the United States and Spain setting the forty-second parallel as the southern boundary between the Oregon area and Mexico. Spain thus gave up her claim to the Oregon Territory.

1820s — The western fur trade began in earnest, reached its

climax during the 1830s and had run its course by the 1840s. Both the British and Americans competed for the fur trade in Oregon.

1824 — The northern boundary of the Oregon Territory is set when Russia agrees to the 54°40′ parallel as Alaska's southern border, thus giving up her claim to the Oregon Territory. Only the U.S. and Britain still claim the area.

— The practice of fur trappers rendezvous began under the American William Henry Ashley. Many of the famous mountain men such as Tom Fitzpatrick, Jim Clyman, Jed Smith, Jim Bridger, Bill Sublette, and Joseph Walker began their work at this time. These and others would serve as pilots for the emigrants of the 1840s.

— Jed Smith, Jim Bridger, Tom Fitzpatrick, Jim Clyman and others traversed the South Pass. The path was now clearly identified.

— Independence Rock was named by Tom Fitzpatrick or other trappers from the Rocky Mountain Fur Company. Father DeSmet will later call the rock "the Great Registry of the Desert" because of all the names carved on it by trappers and emigrants.

1825 — Fort Vancouver was established by the Hudson's Bay Company on the Columbia River near the mouth of the Willamette River. It soon became the fur trade center in the Northwest. By 1830, it had been moved closer to the banks of the river. Dr. John McLoughlin became the Chief Factor and built it into a position of prominence. It was the goal and early re-supply place for the early emigrants once they established their settlements in Oregon. In 1846, McLoughlin resigned from the Hudson's Bay

Company and moved to Oregon City. By 1860 Fort Vancouver's era had ended and by 1866, nothing was left of the fort. Today it is a National Historic Site and parts of it have been reconstructed to serve as a living museum.

1827 — Independence, Missouri, was established and became the "jumping off" place for the Santa Fe Trail in place of Fort Osage. Independence had fine springs and woods. As interest in California and Oregon developed, Independence became the rendezvous place of trail groups following the Santa Fe Trail for a few days, until the trail split and then headed northwest towards the Platte River. For the early emigrants, it would serve as the starting place, but by 1848 it became less important for Oregon travelers as other cities developed further up the Missouri. Today there are a number of trail-related buildings still standing. Independence Square marks the beginning of the Oregon Trail.

— Fort Leavenworth was established as a military post to provide protection for the traders and travelers on the Santa Fe Trail. During the gold rush era of 1849–52, it would serve as another "jumping off" area for the trek west.

1828 — Hiram Scott, a prominent trapper in the Rocky Mountain fur trade, disappeared near present-day Scotts Bluff. William Sublette found his skeleton in 1829, and both the naming of the area for him and the legends concerning the circumstances about his death began. One of the first written records of the legend was by Warren Ferris in 1830, but it was Captain Bonneville's 1832 version that was first published in 1837 by Washington Irving.

1830 — The first ten wagons moved out as part of the Smith-

Jackson-Sublette fur caravan to the rendezvous near Lander, Wyoming. These were supply wagons, not emigrant wagons.

1831 — A group of Nez Perce and Flathead Indians traveled to St. Louis seeking the "white-man's book" that could tell them how to worship the Great Spirit. The *Christian Advocate* printed a "glorified" version about their quest for Christianity, and the various religious groups soon took up their "call" to bring Christianity to the Indians.

1832 — Captain Benjamen Bonneville headed west with wagons along the Platte through the South Pass to the Green River area, and later into Idaho. From a ridge now called Bonneville Point, he is said to have cried, "Le bois! Le bois! Voyez le bois!" at the sight of the forested river valley, from which the present-day river and city take their names — Boise.

   — Hall Jackson Kelley formed the American Society for Encouraging the Settlement of the Oregon Territory. This aroused interest, but no settlements.

1833 — The town of Westport situated near Independence was founded by John C. McCoy. With the development of Westport Landing on the Missouri River, the two areas slowly grow together. Westport Landing was to serve as another of the many "jumping off" places for the trek west. This trail connected to the one from Independence at a point near the present site of New Santa Fe at the Kansas-Missouri line.

1834 — Robert Campbell and about twelve of William Sublette's men built Fort William near the mouth of the Laramie River. It was a rectangle, approximately eighty-by-one-hundred-feet made with fifteen-foot cottonwood logs. A gate was in the center of one wall with its blockhouse and two others in opposite corners. Jim Bridger, Tom Fitzpatrick, and Milton Sublette bought it in 1835 and sold it to the American Fur Company by 1836. It became a brief center for the fur trade and travelers to that area. Fort William was immortalized by Alfred J. Miller in his painting in 1837. In 1841 it was abandoned, probably due to flooding problems and a new fort was constructed — Fort John.

— Nathaniel J. Wyeth began construction of Fort Hall on the Snake river bottom (near present-day Pocatello). It was originally an eighty-foot-square log structure set up for the fur trade business. Wyeth had contracted originally to sell his supplies at the rendezvous, but the mountain men and fur company bought their supplies from Bill Sublette and Wyeth was left holding his. Construction of the trading post or fort seemed like a wise solution. However, competition with the Hudson's Bay Company forced the sale of Fort Hall to the Hudson's Bay Company in 1837. In the following year, the log structure was encased by adobe and then expanded to about eighty-by-one-hundred-twenty-feet. For the emigrants, arrival at Fort Hall represented the completion of the second third of their journey to Oregon, and thus it was a high point. By the late 1840s, the fur trade was declining. The 1850s brought some Indian trouble, and the Hudson's Bay Company abandoned the fort in 1856. It soon fell into disrepair and succumbed to the Snake River floods in 1862. Today, the site of Fort Hall is on the Fort Hall Indian Reservation and is closed to sightseers.

— Jason Lee, Methodist minister, traveled to the Flathead Indians to Christianize them, but decided to keep going to the Willamette to set up a mission there. Interest in Christianizing the Indians and heading for Oregon continued to grow. Also accompaning him was Daniel Lee. The Methodist mission was set up at Salem, Oregon.

— Thomas McKay of the Hudson's Bay Company constructed Fort Boise near the ford of the Snake River below the mouth of the Boise. It was originally of wooden construction, but was encased with adobe by 1839. The fort was built to compete with Nathaniel Wyeth's Fort Hall. It was the adobe fort that most emigrants saw. Like many of the other forts which were built on the river banks, flooding was a constant problem, and by 1853, it was destroyed and abandoned. Today, nothing remains of the fort except a marker where it is thought to have stood.

1836 — Dr. Marcus Whitman, who had gone West previously with Samuel Parker, started west with Henry Spalding to bring Christianity to the Indians. With them were their wives, Narcissa Prentiss Whitman and Eliza Spalding and the first emigrant wagon. These two ladies became the first white women to cross the South Pass. The Whitmans established the Whitman Mission at Waiilatpu, near Walla Walla and the Columbia River. The Oregon emigrants stopped at the mission for rest and supplies, but by the mid-1840s only those emigrants in trouble traveled there. It was the Whitmans who took in the seven Sager children who had been orphaned along the trail in 1844. The mission, opened to the Cayuse Indians, included a gristmill, blacksmith shop, mission house and other buildings. The Spaldings set up their mission further east among the Nez Perce Indians.

1838 — Daniel Lee, a relative of Jason Lee, established the Wascopam Methodist Indian Mission at The Dalles. It was considered by some to be one of the most successful Indian missions in the area. It was occupied until 1847, when it was sold to Dr. Whitman prior to his death in the massacre at his own mission in November 1847. The mission included two houses, barns and stables, gardens, and a schoolhouse. It served also to greet the emigrants after their long journey. Some have said it rendered greater service to the emigrants than Whitman's mission near Walla Walla. Nearby, the wagons were given up for rafting down the Columbia. After 1845, many left The Dalles to head over the Barlow Road to Oregon City.

1838-9 — The Shawnee Methodist Mission was established in Kansas west of the Westport/Independence area. Indian children were sent there to learn English, manual arts, and agriculture. It was also an early stop or camping grounds for the emigrants. Many travelers such as Whitman, Fremont, and Parkman stopped there at the beginning of their journeys. The three major buildings standing today were constructed between 1839 and 1845. The mission was also the location of the first territorial meeting for Kansas in 1855. By 1862, the Shawnee mission closed its doors. Today it is a historical museum that reflects the 1850s period.

1840 — Father Pierre-Jean DeSmet, a Jesuit, moved west to set up missions to bring Christianity to the Indians. He became one of the most famous missionaries of the westward movement. He had earlier set up a mission in the Council Bluffs area that functioned between 1837 and 1841. He would spend thirty-two years working with the Indians of the West and came to be respected by both the natives and whites.

1841 — The first bona fide emigrant wagon company heads west towards Oregon with Thomas Fitzpatrick and Joseph Meek as its guides, and John Bidwell and John Bartleson as its captains. West of Soda Springs near Fort Hall, the party split, some to Oregon and some to California. The migration to Oregon had started.

— Fort John is constructed on the Laramie River to replace the earlier Fort William. It was an adobe structure, rectangular in shape and enclosed an area 123 ft. x 168 ft. It had towers at diagonal ends and two gates. The main gate with a blockhouse was in the middle of one wall, and a smaller one on another. Inside along the walls were numerous buildings. This was the fort the early emigrants called Fort Laramie. This fort was used until it was sold to the army in 1849. The fort was an important point in the emigrants' trek west, as it ended the first third of their trip — an end to the plains, with the mountains soon to begin. Even though Fort John was sold and slowly replaced by the new Fort Laramie, the last portion of it was not taken down until 1862. Today nothing remains of old Fort John.

1842 — Lt. John C. Fremont's exploration expedition guided by Kit Carson heads west along the trail to the Rocky Mountains and South Pass and then in 1843-4, it goes all the way to Oregon. His reports to Congress provide a wealth of geographic information about the area the emigrants will pass through, including convenient mileage figures for the trail. With Charles Preuss, his cartographer, the "Topographical Map of the Road from Missouri to Oregon" was printed and devoured by Congress and the public. Over ten thousand copies of each of his first two reports to Congress were printed. He was the "Pathfinder" to the West. His maps plotted the route, and many emigrants used them. A copy is included later.

— Dr. John McLoughlin, "Lion of the North," Chief Factor of the Hudson's Bay Company, had Oregon City formally platted. Here at the falls of the Willamette was the end to upstream navigation, and power for his sawmill. He had earlier set up a trading center there in 1829, but it was burned. Shortly thereafter, he had his first mill built there. By 1843, the population was about one hundred. Oregon City now served as the "end of the Oregon Trail."

— Dr. Elijah White led a wagon train of thirty wagons and one hundred twelve people west. Acting as pilots or guides at various times were James Coates, Stephen Meek, and Tom Fitzpatrick. Lansford Hastings, a member of the company, later writes one of the early guidebooks for the trail.

— Horace Greeley of the *Tribune* began to write about Oregon and the West. While at first he did not write favorably about the overland trek, he would later. "Manifest Destiny" would be the cry and the lands to the Pacific were the goal. Nothing would come to stand in the way.

1842–3 — Jim Bridger and his partner, Louis Vasquez, constructed their trading post near the Black's Fork of the Green River. Compared with construction of other trading posts or forts, it was a crude, shabby log structure, but served its purpose. During the early years of the trail, and especially for the Mormons, it became a major stopping and re-supply area. Later, emigrants would by-pass it by using the Sublette, Kinney, or Slate Creek cutoffs. Brigham Young purchased Fort Bridger in 1855, but abandoned and burned it in 1857 when friction increased between the Mormons and the U.S. government. The following year, the U.S. Army began to construct the Fort Bridger that presently stands. It was permanently abandoned in 1890. Today, it is a living museum and Wyoming Historic Site.

1843 — The city of St. Joseph was laid out by Joseph Robidoux who had earlier established a trading post there in 1826. Within a few years, "St. Joe" became a major starting point for emigrants. By traveling two more days by steamer up-river from Independence, emigrants could save almost two weeks travel. The Pony Express began here also in 1860.

— This was the year of the "Great Emigration." Dr. Marcus Whitman served as one of the pilots, as did John Gantt, a fur trader. Approximately eight hundred seventy-five people headed west with perhaps seventy-five percent being women and children in as many as two hundred wagons. The West was now a place for families. Two of the most notable emigrants were Peter Burnett who served briefly as captain of a company and Jesse Applegate of the "Cow Column" fame. Burnett would later become governor of California.

— The Oregon Provisional Government was established May 2 at the Champoeg Convention, with Ira L. Babcock presiding as chairman. The vote was 52–50 in favor of the resolution. George Abernethy became the first governor and Oregon City the capital.

1844 — Three major wagon trains head for Oregon, led by

Cornelius Gilliam, Nathan Ford, and Meyer Thorp. Guides included "Black" Harris, Andrew Sublette, and Caleb Greenwood.

— The major route of the Oregon Trail bypasses the Whitman Mission. Black Harris was one of the first to head directly west, continuing along the Umatilla River after leaving the Blue Mountains instead of north to the mission. By 1845, most of the emigrants head west, thereby saving about forty miles and two days travel.

— The Greenwood Cutoff, or what became more popularly known as the Sublette Cutoff, was opened. This headed almost due west from the South Pass area, bypassing the southward dip of the trail towards Fort Bridger, thus saving about seventy-five miles and four days travel. One major difficulty of this cutoff was the lack of water for nearly fifty miles. This was compounded by an error in one of the guidebooks which stated it was dry for only thirty-five miles, and this was quite a shock to many emigrants. Still, many emigrants took the cutoff. For any of you who wish to try the cutoff today, there is a large sign warning you that you *travel at your own risk — Take Heed!*

— The Presidential election and campaign were reflected in the slogans, "Fifty-four, -forty or Fight!" and "All of Oregon or None!" James K. Polk was elected and talks began with Great Britain over the conflicting claims to the Oregon Territory.

1845–6 — Samuel Barlow arrived at The Dalles in Oregon. Concerned with the high tolls charged by those piloting rafts down the Columbia and the treacherous water at the Cascades, he decided to look for a land route to Oregon City. He blazed the route with Joel

Palmer south from The Dalles, then over the Cascade Mountains around Mount Hood to Oregon City. In 1846 Samuel Barlow and Philip Foster chartered the route around Mount Hood as a toll road, thus enabling them to charge other emigrants. On this route was found one of the most difficult sections of the whole trail — Laurel Hill and the "chute." Yet for most emigrants, it was safer than rafting down the Columbia River. During the first year of the Barlow Road's use (1846), one hundred fifty-three wagons and seven hundred people used it. Its usage finally was ended about 1920. The toll for a wagon and team during its early years was five dollars and ten cents per animal. Today, it is still possible to drive on some sections of the Barlow Road and hike on other sections.

1846 — The treaty with Great Britain was signed, agreeing to the forty-ninth parallel as the northern boundary of the United States from the Rocky Mountains to the Pacific Ocean. The southern portion of the contested Oregon Territory is officially part of the United States.

— The first Fort Kearny was established at what became Nebraska City in 1854. Yet within two years, the fort was abandoned for the one built out on the Platte. Some emigrants continued to use the area, and Nebraska City had its heyday for trail traffic in the late 1850s.

— Congress approved "an Act to provide for raising a regiment of Mounted Riflemen, and for establishing military stations on the route to Oregon." The Mexican War, however, delayed action on this until 1848–9. Osborne Cross would serve as quartermaster and write his famous journal in 1849.

— The Applegate Trail was opened and gave entrance to Oregon from the south. It followed the California Trail cutoff from the Fort Hall area into Nevada along the Humbolt River and then northwest into Oregon. The emigrants on this trail were reported to have experienced more Indian problems than those on the regular northern route. This was the route used by the emigrants killed at Tule Lake the following year.

1847 — Brigham Young entered the Great Salt Lake Valley and the Mormon "Promised Land" was founded. The years of the mass Mormon migration began. Most of the "Saints" would follow the Platte River on its northern bank, crossing over at Fort Laramie. This route came to be called "The Mormon Trail."

— Brigham Young returned and other Mormon emigrants moved into the Omaha-Kanesville-Council Bluffs area. This area served as a supply and outfitting area for both Mormon and Gentile emigrants. It was in this area that the Mormons set up their now-sacred "winter quarters." By the early 1850s, most of the "Saints" had left the Council Bluffs area, and by the late 1850s, it had replaced those cities further downstream as the major starting point for the westward trek. It has been estimated that nearly thirty percent of the pre-1867 emigrants used this area. With the coming of the Union Pacific in 1864, emigrant wagon traffic dropped off.

— A measles epidemic struck the settlers and the Cayuse Indians near the Whitman Mission. While the Whitmans were fairly successful in treating the settlers, the Cayuse, having no resistance to it, died quickly. Feeling that the Whitmans were responsible a band of Cayuse entered the Whitman house on

November 29 and killed the Whitmans, the Sager boys, and nine others. This massacre touched off the Cayuse Indian War. It also ended the mission's role, but the outcry resulting from it increased official interest in Oregon.

1848 — Oregon became an official U.S. Territory.

— Lieutenant Woodbury began construction of Fort Kearny near Grand Island on the Platte River. It was first called Fort Childs, but almost immediately, the War Department renamed it Fort Kearny. The fort is one of the few along the trail that was built specifically to protect the emigrants and was located near where all the various routes from the "jumping off" places converged. It served as a major supply post for both the military and the emigrants. Lieutenant Woodbury had cottonwood trees planted around the parade grounds, and a few of these trees still stand today. During the period of Indian trouble, Fort Kearny played a significant role. As peace returned to the Central Plains and the railroad came in the late 1860s, the center of military activity shifted to other forts. By 1871 Fort Kearny was abandoned and by 1875, it was gone. Today there is a reconstruction of part of it and a museum. It is a Nebraska State Historical Park.

1849–52 — While cholera took its toll throughout the history of the trail, the years 1849, 1850, and 1852 saw it in epidemic form, and it took a massive toll. Some companies reportedly lost two-thirds of their members, while others were lucky and lost only a few. Cholera was on both sides of the Platte, but seemed worse on the south side. It was also more of a problem along the trail until it reached Fort Laramie. McCollum wrote, "The road from Indepen-

dence to Ft. Laramie is a graveyard." The emigrants'
remedy for it was a solution of cornmeal and raw
whiskey.

— These were also the years of the major California
Gold Rush traffic. Emigrants followed the Oregon
Trail until near Soda Springs or south of Fort Hall
at the Raft River, where the trails branched off to
California.

1849 — Robidoux established a small trading post and blacksmith shop near today's Scotts Bluff, in the area
called Robidoux Pass. It was abandoned after 1851
and by 1853 had fallen into ruin. This pass was the
major route taken by the early Oregon emigrants
and used until nearby Mitchell Pass was developed.

— This was the year the army officially took action to
safeguard the Oregon Trail. The Regiment of
Mounted Riflemen, comprised of ten companies and
additional infantry companies, was sent west along
the trail to man the military forts. Osborne Cross
served as quartermaster for this expedition and made
his reports. Col. W. W. Loring left Fort Leavenworth
and headed for Oregon City, leaving detachments
at Fort Kearny and Fort Laramie. Proceding west,
he established a new post near Fort Hall called Cantonment Loring, and then headed for Oregon. In
1850, Cantonment Loring was abandoned due to
problems of spring and flooding. Detachments were
sent from Fort Vancouver and Oregon City to build
another fort on the Columbia River at The Dalles.
The establishment of the military along the trail
led to an increase in traffic due to the need for
supplies, reinforcements, periodic rotation, and the
establishment of additional posts and forts in later
years. For the first time, soldiers were sent to guard
a wagon company on the trail to California.

— The military post of Fort Laramie was established. Pierre Chouteau of the former American Fur Company sold Fort John to Lt. Daniel Woodbury for the U.S. government. Major Sanderson was placed in command of the newly-established garrison and immediately began an expansion of the fort area. Old Bedlam and the Sutler's Store were constructed and are still standing today. During the years of expansion, old Fort John was torn down to make room for newer buildings. The fort was abandoned in 1890. As mentioned earlier the emigrants' arrival at Fort Laramie signaled the end to the first third of their journey west. Today, it is still a major stop and resting place for those traveling along the trail. It is a National Historic Site and has an exellent living museum where one can spend many profitable hours.

— Benoni M. Hudspeth on his way to California led his party west from Soda Springs, instead of heading northwest to Fort Hall and then southwest to the Raft River, where the older California Trail branched off. His new route joined the old California Trail later on the Raft River. This was the beginning of the Hudspeth Cutoff.

1850 — Fort Dalles was established by Captain Tucker on the Columbia near the Methodist Mission at The Dalles. Lewis and Clark had earlier built their Fort Rock near the same area. First, the fort was known as Camp Dunn, then Fort Dunn, and by 1855, Fort Dalles. Its main function as a military post was to protect the emigrants on the Oregon Trail. In 1867 the fort was abandoned. Today, only the Surgeon's Quarters remains as a museum.

— Monthly contract mail service was begun by Judge

Samuel Woodson and James Brown from Independence to Fort Bridger and Salt Lake along the trail.

1851 — Mitchell Pass at Scotts Bluff began to be used by emigrant wagons. However the earliest documented use of the pass was in 1834 in the journals of Jason Lee, John Townsend, and Nathaniel Wyeth. By 1852, half of the emigrant traffic used Mitchell Pass, thus bypassing the first-used Robidoux Pass. Mitchell Pass is today the location of the Oregon Trail Museum, and many original William Henry Jackson paintings are there. It has a small living museum and a visitor can walk the same route used by wagons over a century ago.

— Just west of Scotts Bluff at Horse Creek, one of the largest Indian treaty councils was held. Over ten thousand Indians from twelve plains nations attended. The Indians agreed to cease their sometimes troublesome behavior in return for respect of their tribal lands and fees for crossing their lands. Unfortunately, like most other agreements, this was broken within three years. This treaty is sometimes referred to as the "first Fort Laramie treaty."

1854 — The "Grattan Massacre" happened. This unfortunate incident which occurred near Fort Laramie was to be the precurser of the Indian problem which developed into the Indian Wars of the 1860s. It was only three years after the historic Fort Laramie Treaty. The incident primarily dealt with the army and Indians, although an emigrant was involved at its beginning. An emigrant's cow wandered off into a friendly Indian village, but instead of pursuing the cow, the emigrant went to Fort Laramie. There, Lieutenant Grattan, twenty-nine others, and a field piece set out to get the "stolen" cow back. In the meantime, a visiting Indian had killed the cow, and it had been eaten. Grattan arrived and tried in vain to find out the Indians responsible. Unable to do and unwilling to accept a horse in place of the cow, Grattan aimed his cannon at one of the Indian lodges and opened fire. After the soldiers stopped, the Indians retaliated. When the fighting was over, the Brule Chief Bear and other Indians had been killed, along with all of the military force except for one who escaped to tell of the "massacre." The fat was now in the fire. Indians sporadically raided other nearby areas during the next year, and the military stepped up its patrols and would seek its "revenge."

— One day after the "Grattan Massacre," the "Alexander Ward Wagon Train Massacre" happened near Fort Boise. This was one of the very few emigrant wagon train attacks during this period of the Oregon Trail. A band of Snake Indians attempted to steal a horse. One of the emigrants shot an Indian and a battle resulted. Of the twenty emigrants, only two survived. They were boys whom the Indians thought were dead. The military and others reacted swiftly and indiscriminantly, which only increased Indian hostilities. As a result, travel became more dangerous, and the Indian trouble contributed to the decision of the Hudson's Bay Company to close Fort Hall and not to rebuild Fort Boise.

1855 — This was the year the military would avenge the prior year's massacres. Major Haller moved out of Fort Dalles with one hundred fifty soldiers towards Fort Boise. There, he held council with Indians in the area and seized four Indians involved in the Ward encounter. One was killed trying to escape, and the other three were hanged near the site of the massacre.

— A treaty council was held near Walla Walla with most of the major tribes inhabiting the lands east of the Cascades from Washington, northeast Oregon, and Idaho. Over five thousand Indians including the Nez Perce, Umatillas, Cayuse, Walla Walla, Palouse, and others were present. Most of Indians west of the Cascades had already "given up" their lands, and now more lands were needed for settlement. Some of the Indians, sensing the futility of opposition, and others hoping to live in peace with the whites, agreed to yield some of their lands and move onto reservations. Trouble started almost immediately after the signing, as whites moved in before arrangements were made for the establishment of the reservations. Fighting erupted, but for the Indians, it was too late.

— In September, after the emigrant season had passed, General Harney found and engaged an encampment of Indians under Little Thunder at Blue Waters, north of Ash Hollow. While there is still some disagreement concerning the specific events, it appears Little Thunder tried to talk to General Harney. It seemed Harney would have little or nothing to do with the talk, and within a short time, the battle was engaged. The Indians lost eighty-six women, children, and braves, the military only four. The "Grattan Massacre" was avenged!

1858 — The army began to rebuild Fort Bridger and by 1859, twenty-nine buildings had been constructed. It continued to serve as a military post until 1890, with only a two-year period (1878–80) when it was deactivated. Today, nothing remains of Jim Bridger's original trading post, but many of the buildings of the military era are standing. It is a living museum and State Historic Site.

— Fort Caspar was established near one of the crossings of the North Platte River in central Wyoming. Louis Guinard established a trading post and erected a bridge across the Platte near the location of the earlier Mormon ferries and the Reshaw bridge. The post was called originally the Mormon Ferry Post or Platte Bridge Station, until named Fort Caspar in 1865 after Lt. Caspar Collins who was killed there in the line of duty. In 1867, the fort was abandoned when Fort Fetterman was established, and both the fort and the bridge were burned by the Indians. Today, there is a fine reconstruction of the fort and museum on its former site.

1859 — The Lander Road and Cutoff was built by Frederick Lander specifically for emigrant use. It headed northwest from the Burnt Ranch east of South Pass and met the older Oregon Trail east of Fort Hall, thus saving about one hundred miles. Because of its construction late in the period of migration, it did not play a major role in Oregon's early history.

— Oregon enters the Union as a state.

These then were some of the important events in the early development of the Oregon Trail. Starting about 1849, the nature of the Oregon Trail changed with the coming of the California Gold Rush and the Forty-Niners, the military presense, increased disease, the physical improvements such as ferries and bridges, the appearance of steamboats on the Columbia River during the 1850s, and the beginnings of the Indian troubles. With the 1860s came more changes — increased settlements, the Pony Express, telegraph, stagecoaches and then the railroads. These newer modes of communications and transportation used the general route of the trail, often running parallel to it, and frequently the tracks were laid right over the trail. While the railroads did not kill the use of the trail immediately, they did alter its need. The Indian wars of the 1860s also had an impact on the trail. However, they were not directly related to the trail itself, but rather changes in culture and the treatment of the Indians by the whites.

Part II
Wagon Wheels Over Plains and Mountains

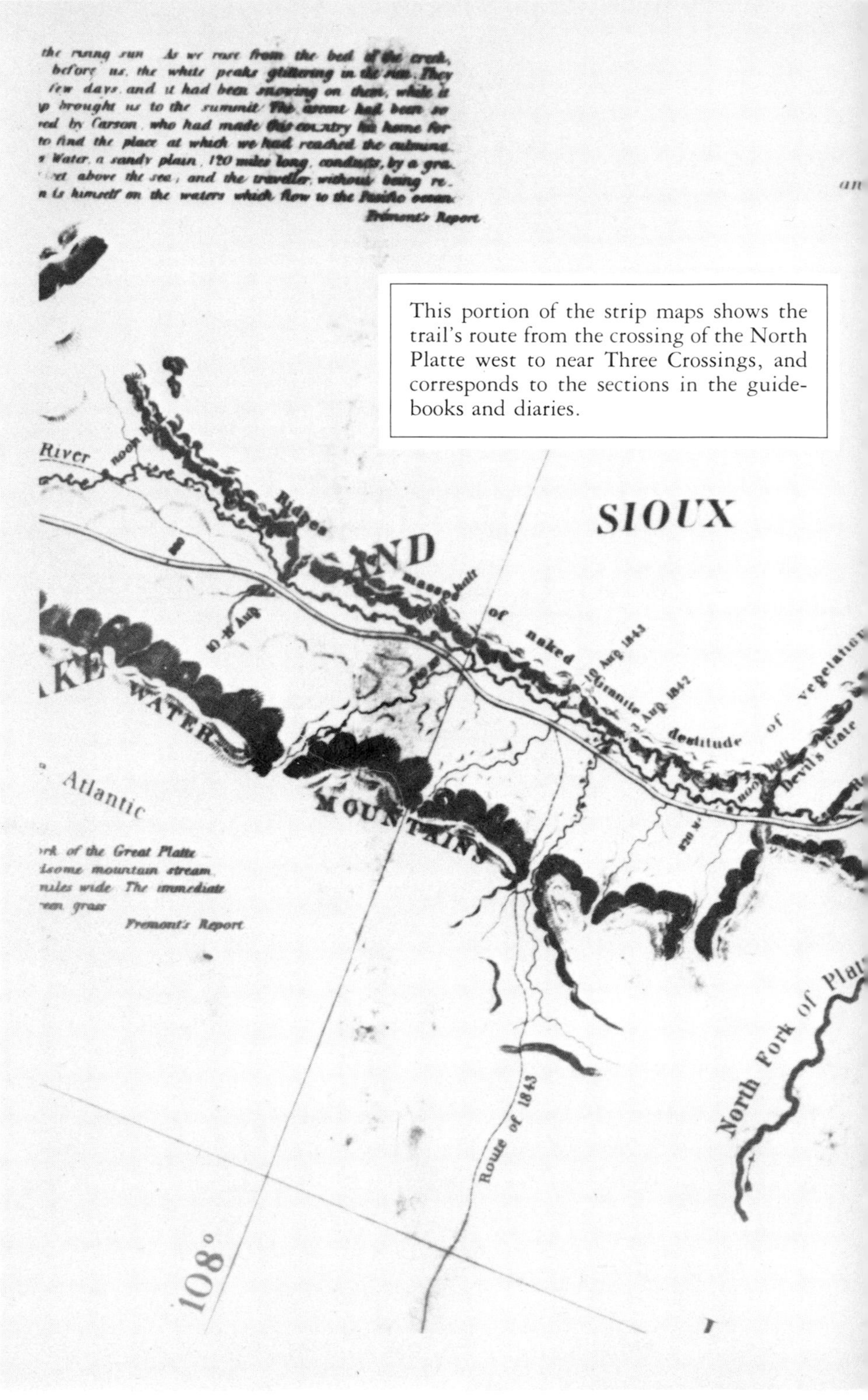

the rising sun. As we rose from the bed of the creek,
before us, the white peaks glittering in the sun. They
few days, and it had been snowing on them, while it
up brought us to the summit. The ascent had been so
red by Carson, who had made this country his home for
to find the place at which we had reached the culmina
s Water, a sandy plain, 120 miles long, conducts, by a gra
feet above the sea; and the traveller, without being re
n is himself on the waters which flow to the Pacific ocean.
Fremont's Report

This portion of the strip maps shows the
trail's route from the crossing of the North
Platte west to near Three Crossings, and
corresponds to the sections in the guidebooks and diaries.

SIOUX

River

AKE WATER

Atlantic

rk of the Great Platte
some mountain stream
miles wide. The immediate
een grass
Fremont's Report

ND

of naked

Granite Aug 1842

destitute

of vegetation

Devil's Gate

MOUNTAINS

Route of 1843

North Fork of Platte

108°

SECTION IV

From the field notes and journal of Capt. J C Fremont

from sketches and notes made on the ground by his assistant Charles

Compiled by Charles Preuss. 1846

By order of the Senate of the United States

SCALE — 10 MILES TO THE INCH

Lithogr. by E. Weber & Co. Baltimore

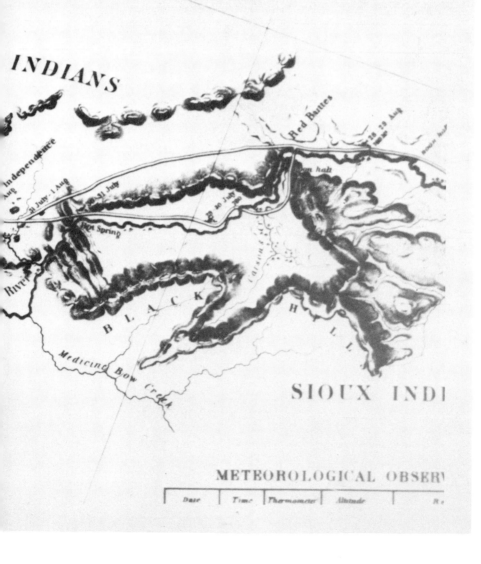

INDIANS

Red Buttes

Independence

31 July. 1 Aug

31 July

Hot Spring

BLACK

River

Medicine Bow Creek

H L L

SIOUX INDI

METEOROLOGICAL OBSERV

Date	Time	Thermometer	Altitude		R

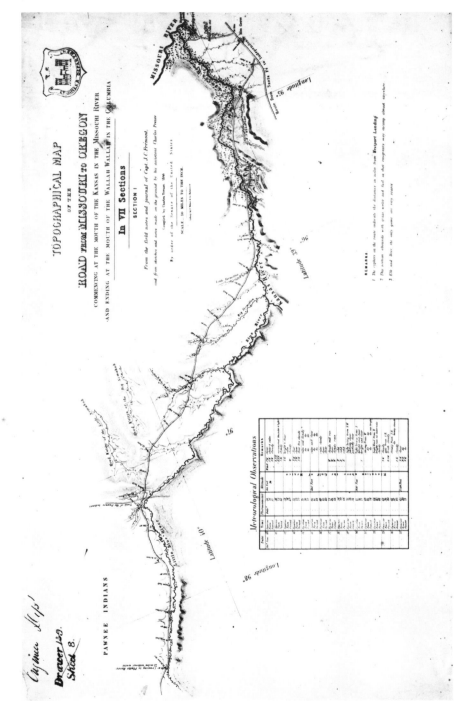

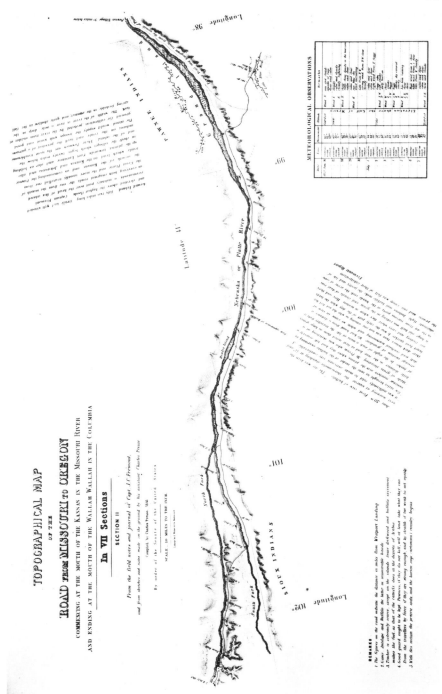

TOPOGRAPHICAL MAP
of the
ROAD from MISSOURI to OREGON
COMMENCING AT THE MOUTH OF THE KANSAS IN THE MISSOURI RIVER
AND ENDING AT THE MOUTH OF THE WALLAH WALLAH IN THE COLUMBIA

In VII Sections
SECTION II

From the field notes and journal of Capt. J.C. Frémont,
and from sketches and notes made on the ground by his assistant Charles Preuss

Compiled by Charles Preuss 1846

By order of the Senate of the United States

SCALE 10 MILES TO THE INCH

METEOROLOGICAL OBSERVATIONS

REMARKS
1. The figures on the road indicate the distances in miles from Westport Landing
2. Game - Antelope and Buffalo the latter is innumerable herds
3. Timber is extremely scarce except on the islands, heart driftwood and buffalo excrement
4. Water the fluid in the streams does in the deserts of betters
5. Good ground ought to be kept Provisos, if they do not kill well at least take what they can
6. From the travellers by force if they are strong enough and by stealth if too weak to act openly
7. With this notion the prairie ends and the barren sage settlement country begins

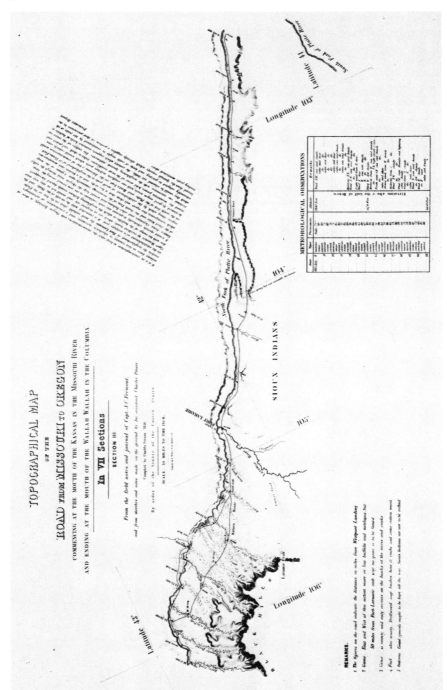

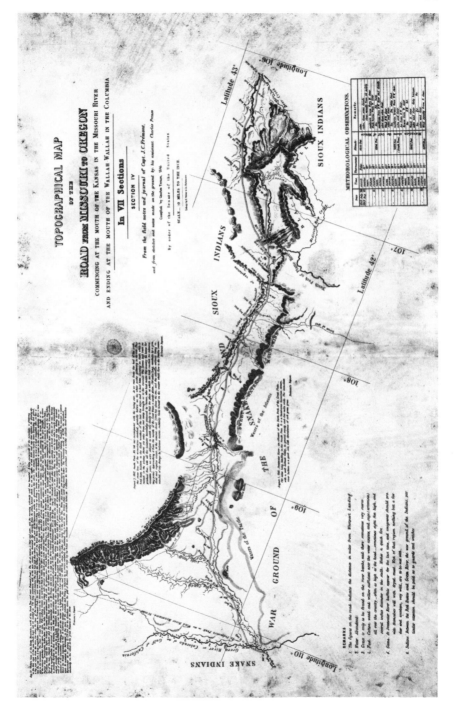

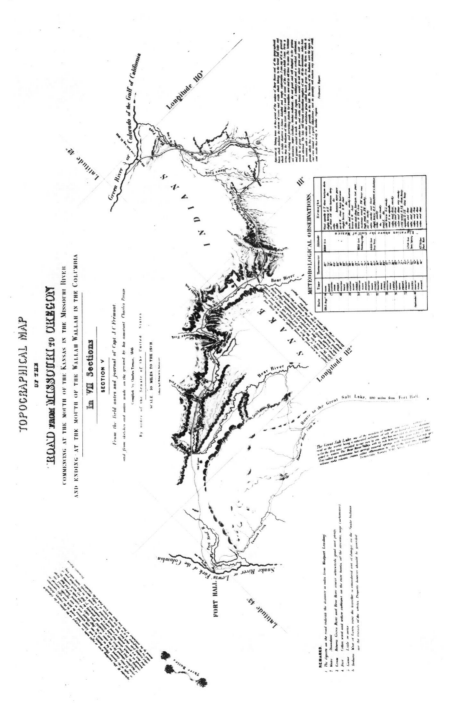

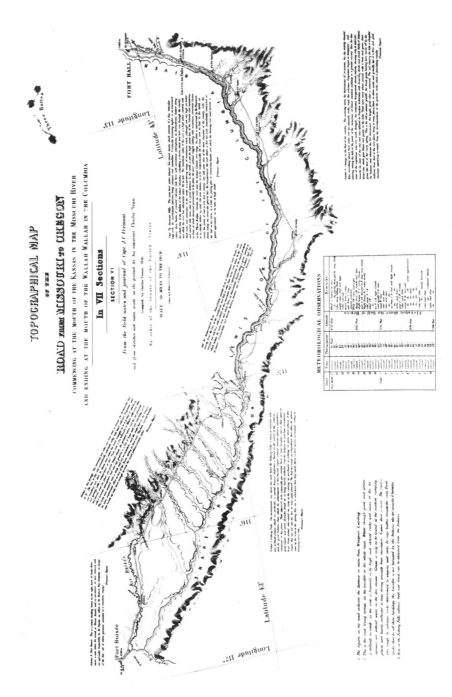

TOPOGRAPHICAL MAP
OF THE
ROAD FROM MISSOURI TO OREGON
COMMENCING AT THE MOUTH OF THE KANSAS IN THE MISSOURI RIVER
AND ENDING AT THE MOUTH OF THE WALLAH WALLAH IN THE COLUMBIA

In VII Sections

SECTION VI

From the field notes and journal of Capt. J.C. Fremont
and from sketches and notes made on the ground by his assistant Charles Preuss

Compiled by Charles Preuss 1846

By order of the Senate of the United States

SCALE 10 MILES TO THE INCH

METEOROLOGICAL OBSERVATIONS

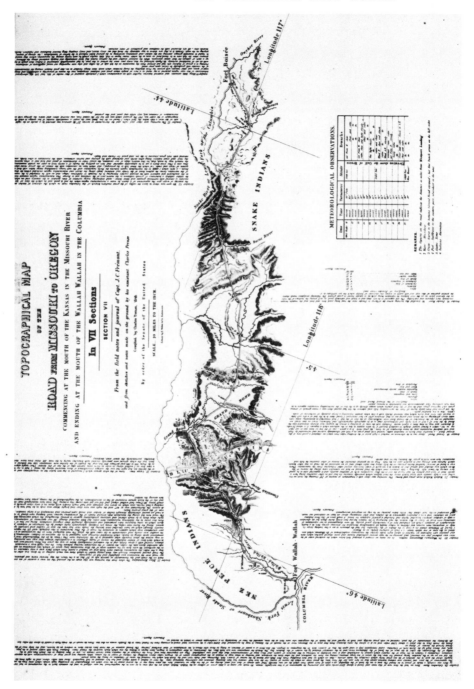

The Emigrant Guides

THE PAGES that follow are from Johnson and Winter's 1846 guide *Route Across the Rocky Mountains* and Clayton's 1847 *The Latter-Day Saints Emigrant's Guide*. The sections from both guidebooks cover the overland route after crossing the North Platte in the vicinity of present-day Casper and the Red Buttes to the Sweetwater and Independence Rock, and then toward the Three Crossings and South Pass. As you read, note the improved quality and detail provided in Clayton's guide. Maj. Osborne Cross wrote in his journal on August 3, 1849:

> "On the route to the South Pass, I would have wanted no better guide than the Mormon Guide Book, which I found to be very exact throughout the distance. It has noted down every hill, valley, and stream you meet with, stating with great precision the several points where good encampments could be reached, and the distances between each place. We had but a few along, and it is hoped, for the benefit of emigrants, they may become more freely circulated."

In fact, Clayton's guide was so good that sections of later guidebooks, such as *Horn's Overland Guide* (1852) and other guides, were partially based on it. Many emigrants also copied sections of the guidebooks right into the appropriate sections of their own diaries.

The Fremont-Preuss strip map included earlier corresponds also to the same area described in the guidebooks. However, Fremont crossed the North Platte south at Red Buttes and traveled along the river, whereas the emigrants drove overland from that area. Therefore, his map includes only the overland section, but does not show any details on it. Once at Independence Rock, they all followed the same general route along the Sweetwater River to South Pass. There were seven strip maps in the Fremont-Preuss series showing the route to Oregon. Each having about two hundred fifty miles to the sheet. The scale was ten miles to the inch. For those emigrants who had copies, the trek to Oregon must have seemed much safer. Over the years, the trail developed into many twisted and parallel routes as the emigrants tried to find shorter, safer, or easier paths.

Most of the emigrants did not keep diaries of their journey. They were either too occupied with the rigors of the trail during the day or too tired at night or during breaks to write. Many of those who did write had lapses in their narratives which were often explained later by illness or exhaustion. However, most emigrants did not write because they probably did not see the need for a diary of their venture. Merrill Mattes has estimated that an average of one in about two hundred fifty emigrants kept some written records. Also, others that were kept were undoubtedly lost or destroyed on the trip, and some thrown away years later or still stored in some forgotten trunk in an attic.

However, a great number of diaries have been located and a few "new" old ones have been located recently. The diaries of the emigrants varied as much as the emigrants themselves. Some were very brief accounts, while others included a wealth of information describing in detail the people, places, and events. Some copies provided by the Oregon Historical Society are included here, they all describe their journey from the different crossing areas of the North Platte near present-day Casper, Wyoming, west to Independence Rock and along the valley of the Sweetwater. In them may be found many of the realities of the trail experience as mentioned at the beginning of the book: the braided changing nature of the trail's route; use of guidebooks; awe at the natural wonders; sickness; contact with the Indians; problems associated with water, firewood, grazing and weather; evidence of death; accidents; buffalo; near breakdowns; home remedies; emigrant crime and justice; family fights; and emigrant philosophy. Velina Williams went to Oregon in 1853; Henry Allyn in 1853; and Enoch Conyers in 1852. It should be noted that this section of the trail, while generally typical, was not as harsh as other sections further west.

For further comparison with the pictures that also correspond to the same section of the trail, turn to page 106 starting with Jackson's painting of Fort Caspar and continue on until page 118 ending with Jackson's painting of the Three Crossings. It was in the same manner that the author used on his various trips west — maps, guidebooks, diaries, and photos and drawings all spread out in the car. At times, it was difficult to coordinate them all, but it made the trail more understandable and interesting.

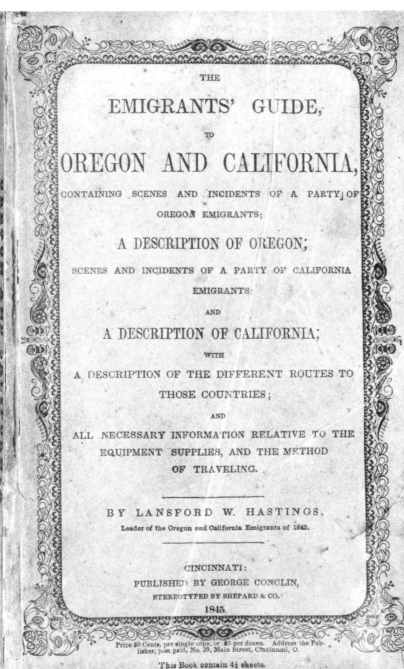

THE

EMIGRANTS' GUIDE,

TO

OREGON AND CALIFORNIA,

CONTAINING SCENES AND INCIDENTS OF A PARTY OF
OREGON EMIGRANTS;

A DESCRIPTION OF OREGON;

SCENES AND INCIDENTS OF A PARTY OF CALIFORNIA
EMIGRANTS:

AND

A DESCRIPTION OF CALIFORNIA;

WITH

A DESCRIPTION OF THE DIFFERENT ROUTES TO
THOSE COUNTRIES;

AND

ALL NECESSARY INFORMATION RELATIVE TO THE
EQUIPMENT SUPPLIES, AND THE METHOD
OF TRAVELING.

BY LANSFORD W. HASTINGS.

Leader of the Oregon and California Emigrants of 1842.

CINCINNATI:
PUBLISHED BY GEORGE CONCLIN,
STEREOTYPED BY SHEPARD & CO.
1845.

Price 50 Cents, per single copy, or $5 per dozen.   Address the Pub-
lisher, post paid, No. 39, Main Street, Cincinnati, O.

This Book contain 4¼ sheets.

The cover for Hastings' *The Emigrants' Guide to Oregon and California.*

	MILES.	Total.	
			wood and grass. Here there are two roads, one following the river, and the other leaving it to the right. That will be preferable which has been least traveled, on account of grass.
The North Fork, -	55	761	This is by the road which leaves the river. Through the Black Hills, there are, in the Spring season, numerous small streams which afford water, a great deal of wood, and grass sufficient for several companies. In this distance, the streams are never more than six miles apart.
The crossing, -	30	791	From the point where the two roads again unite, the trail follows the North Fork to the crossing, never leaving it far. In the bottoms of the stream, there is grass sufficient for camps, and an inexhaustable quantity of wood. The River here, at this season, can generally be forded. If it be high, recourse must be had to rafting, unless emigrants are otherwise provided. Timber is not wanting.
Water,	16	807	Immediately after crossing the Platte, the trail leaves the river entirely, and bears to the right, over a high and uneven country, which affords very little of either wood, water, or grass; and until it reaches Sweet Water, a small river tributary to the North Fork, the most of the water is impregnated with some kind of salts, which render it worse than disagreeable. At this place, there is a spring, and a channel, in which the water sometimes flows. Water salt. Grass scarce. No wood.
Salt Sink, -	10	817	Here, immediately on the trail, the water is salt, and there is scarcely any grass; but green spots may be seen to the right among the hills, where there is excellent grass, and springs of good water. They are five or six hundred yards from the road. Great caution must be observed, to keep out of the sinks, which are numerous, dangerous, and deceptive. No wood.
Willow Springs, -	7	824	Excellent water, some willow brush, and good grass, for a few companies.
Large marsh,	2	826	Water and grass for a few companies. No wood. A small branch flows from this marsh, along which there is some grass. The trail follows it a few miles.
Crooked creek, -	11	837	But little grass, and no wood.
Independence Rock,	8	845	This is on the bank of Sweet Water, along which there is good grass, but not much wood.
Grand Pass, -	97	942	This is to some large and excellent springs, a few miles beyond the head of Sweet Water, and near the summit of the Pass through the Rocky Mountains, (South Pass.) From the In-

This page of Johnson and Winter's Guidebook, 1846, follows the trail with the crossing of the North Platte at mile 791 and continues to the (South Pass) Grand Pass at mile 942.

Clayton's Emigrant Guide — 1847

PROMINENT POINTS AND REMARKS.	Dist. miles.	From W Qrs. miles	From C of G S L miles
Creek, two feet wide. - - -	1½	640	391
No place to camp.			
Muddy creek, 5 feet wide, 1½ feet deep.	1	641	890
No chance to camp.			
2 ravines, near together: Lat. 42° 51′ 44″.	8	644	887
Opposite here there is a fording place, where companies generally have forded the river.			
Creek five feet wide. - - -	3	647	384
Abundance of fish, early in the season, but little grass, and no timber.			
Upper Platte ferry and ford. - -	1½	648½	382½
Plenty of feed and some timber on both sides the river (See Note 4.) Lat. 42° 50′ 18″. Altitude 4,875 feet.			
Road turns south, and rises a long hill. -	7	655½	375½
Ascent gradual. Many singular looking rocks on the south side. Descent rough and crooked. Towards the foot, road very uneven.			
Mineral spring and lake. - - -	5½	661	370
Considered poisonous. No bad taste to the water, unless the cattle trample in it. In that case it becomes black, and is doubtless poisonous. No timber near.			
Rock avenue and steep descent. - -	7½	668½	362½
The road here passes between high rocks, forming a kind of avenue or gateway, for a quarter of a mile.			
Alkali swamps and springs. - -	2	670½	360½
This ought to be avoided as a camping ground—it is a small valley, surrounded by high bluffs. The land exceeding miry, and smells bad. There is a creek of good water north-west. No timber and little grass. Next mile, rough road.			
Small stream of clear spring water. -	4	674½	356½
Good camping place. Plenty of grass, but no wood.			
"Willow Spring." - - - -	2¾	677¼	353¾
About three rods west of the road, at the foot of willow bushes. Water cold and good—grass plenty, but creek some miry.			
"Prospect Hill," (summit.) - -	1	678¼	352¾
Pleasant view of the surrounding country, to the Sweet Water mountains.			
Bad slough. - - - - -	3¼	681½	349½
Plenty of grass, but little water. A mile further is a hill, both steep ascending and descending.			
Creek, 300 yards south of road. - -	1¾	683½	347¾
Plenty of grass, but no wood.			
Small creek, left of the road. - -	2½	685¾	345¼
Grass plentiful, but doubtful for water, and no wood. The road runs alongside this creek for half a mile.			
Grease-wood creek, 6 feet wide 1 ft. deep.	1½	687½	343½
Very little grass, and no fuel but wild sage. Road from here to the Sweet Water sandy, and very heavy.			
Alkali springs and lakes. - - -	6½	693¾	337¼
Here gather your Saleratus from a lake, west of the road. Land swampy, and smells bad. Water poisonous.			
"Sweet-water river," 8 rods wide, 2 ft. deep. - - - - -	4¼	698	333

This page shows the crossing of the North Platte at mile 648½ and continues along the trail to the Sweetwater at mile 698. The reason for the different mileage marker when compared to Johnson & Winter's Guide is that they had different starting places.

Clayton's Emigrant Guide — 1847

PROMINENT POINTS AND REMARKS.	Dist. miles.	From W Qrs. miles.	From C of G S L miles.
Independence Rock and ford. - - On the north side of the river—about six hundred yards long. and a hundred and twenty wide, composed of hard Granite. (See Note 5.)	¾	698¾	332¼
Devil's Gate. - - - - - A little west from the road. The river here passes between perpendicular rocks four hundred feet high.— This is a curiosity worthy of a traveler's notice.	5¼	704	327
Creek two feet wide. - - - Not good to cross. The road runs near the river banks for ten miles after this.	½	704½	326½
Creek, 6 feet wide. - - - Good to cross. Water and grass plenty, but lacks timber. You will find grass all along on the banks of the river, but very little wood.	½	705	326
Deep ravine and creek. - - - Plenty of grass and water, but no wood.	6½	711½	319¾
Deep ravine and creek. - - - Doubtful for water.	¾	712	319
Road leaves the river : Lat. 42° 28′ 25″. Road after this, sandy and heavy, and passes over a high bluff. Land barren for seven and a half miles. (See Note 6.)	3	715	316
Alkali Lake. - - - - - On the left of the road.	½	715½	315½
Sage creek. - - - - - No grass. High banks. Doubtful for water, but Wild Sage plentiful. One and three-quarter miles further you arrive on the river banks again.	4¾	720¼	310¾
Creek, three feet wide. - - - Doubtful for water, but the road runs close to the river.	4	724¼	306¾
High gravelly bluff. - - - - Left of the road, and a very good place to camp.	1¼	725½	305½
Bitter-cotton-wood creek. - - - Doubtful for water and grass. Some timber on it. After this, the road leaves the river for six miles.	1½	727	304
Road arrives at the river. - - -	6¼	733¼	297¾
Leave the old road and ford the river. - By fording here, the road is shorter, and you avoid much very heavy, sandy road. Lat. 42° 31′ 20″.	¼	733½	297½
Road turns between the rocky ridges. - After this, you ford the river twice—but it is easily forded. Then the river leaves the river again.	1½	735	296
Ford No. 4—good camping place. - After this, the road leaves the river again, and you will probably find no water fit to drink for sixteen and a half miles.	8	743	288
Ice Spring. - - - - - This is on a low, swampy spot of land on the right of the road. Ice may generally be found, by digging down about two feet. There are two alkali lakes a little further.	5¾	748¾	282¼
Alkali springs. - - - - -	¼	749	282

This page continues the journey starting at Independence Rock following along the valley of the Sweetwater passed Three Crossings which is at mile 733½ to 735. These crossings allowed the emigrant to avoid the Deep Sand Route.

Diaries

Henry Allyn started the trail at "Cainsville," Iowa. His company passed the upper ferry area on June 24, 1853 and was near the Three Crossings and Deep Sand route by June 29.

June 24, Friday — We start on with an intention of stopping when we came to better grass if it should hurt Betsey too bad to drive. After trying it she concludes that we can drive on. We pass the upper and last ferry on Platte, where the emigration all travel the same road as fas as S. Pass. Came 14 miles. Camp a mile from river, with no fuel but sage and scant of grass. Road thronged with emigrants before and behind us all day. Directly after stopping the two Johns go out to kill some game. About sunset they come in with a young antelope. Get a good mess of milk from the drovers. Betsey gets some better.

June 25, Saturday — After breakfast on antelope veal, we resume our journey. The road forked near our camping place. The new fork leaves the river and is destitute of any but poison water for 20 miles. The other continues up the Platte for 10 miles. We take the old road and when we came to the place of our final departure we water the mules, fill our cans and took leave of our old friend and took up over the hills. We had a rough road for a few miles, but at length it became more even and level and spread out to considerable distance between the peaks and left plenty of space for the road to pass between. At length we arrived at the Willow Springs, where the road comes together again and where we had intended camping. It has been a noted camping place on account of the water, fuel and grass. But we found the grass all pastured out, the willows all consumed, and teams and people enough there to use the water about as fast as it came from its fountain. So we watered and continued on our course, with an intention of finding grass if no other accommodation. We ascended Prospect Hill, which commenced at Willow Springs. When we arrived at the summit, about 1½ miles, the country opens on a level plain for several miles and then another range of high peaks and ridges present themselves. Toward evening the wind arose and blew quite a gale. We whirled the wagons around to stand endwise to the wind, when the rain began to fall in torrents. But the wind soon subsided, the rains ceased and we had quite a pleasant evening. By prospecting a little we found pretty good grass and having some water in our cans and the mules having been watered at Willow Springs, we conclude to encamp, having plenty of sage for fuel. In the vicinity of Willow Springs there were many dead cattle and horses, which I suppose had drank too freely of the alkali lakes along the road. A sad accident happened today to a man near us. He was pulling his revolver out from the wagon, which had been stowed away among other things, and it got hitched and sprung the lock, discharged and nearly ruined one arm. Betsey is some better, but is yet very bad. Came 22 miles.

June 26, Sabbath — Not having accommodations here, we start on this morning. Country about the same for some miles, the soil a light gray, which is a mixture of gravel, sand and clay. Cross several beautiful streams which were fed by springs. At length we descend into a valley, and soon arrive at Sweetwater, a branch of the Platte. Found a great concourse of emigrants there. We continue up the river and pass Independence Rock which is a little below the lower ford. This rock is a great curiosity. Its form is an oblong cone, lying N. E. and S. W. Its S. W. end reaches near to the river. It is perfectly bare of vegetation and is probably 100 feet high and very steep. The guide book says it is 6 or 700 yards long and 120 to 150 yards wide. Devil's Gate is just above us. We camp about half way between it and the rock. Guide book says, "This is a curiosity worthy the traveler's notice; the rocks are 400 feet high and perpendicular, through which the Sweetwater forces its way. The best view is from the east end of it, into which you can go some distance." Betsey is very sick this P. M. Came 19 miles. Yesterday and today we pass much alkali water. High, steep and ragged rocky ridges appear on every hand, running seemingly at random in every direction. We don't cross the river tonight on account of getting better grass, as nearly all the emigration that we have found here have crossed over to camp tonight.

June 27, Monday — Very windy last night, so that we were apprehensive for our safety and the wind continues all day from N. W. It spit some snow, sleet and rain. Cold as January. Lay by today on account of Betsey's illness, who is yet very bad. We suffer much with cold today. James and John P. this morning take an excursion out to the mountain and visited the Devil's Gate. As it was open, they walked in it some distance. For as a general thing he keeps all his gates open. It is a great curiosity. They kill a curlew and return. In the P. M., J. W. and F. D. visit the gate, etc. We have no fuel but sage to make fire, and that rather scarce at this place. The road is filled with emigrants and droves passing us all day. This country, they say, is claimed by the Crow Indians. We have not seen many yet and what few we have are friendly and sociable.

June 28, Tuesday — We start this morning and cross the ford of Sweetwater, with an intention of stopping as soon as we could find better accommodations for camping, provided that Betsey could not bear the jolting. The road being generally good and smooth today, that she did not complain much and we continued on till regular camping time, driving rather slow. Cross two or three handsome streams, falling into Sweetwater. Close by and a little above the Devil's Gate is a little cluster of cabins, occupied. I suppose, by the Mormons as a trading depot. They likewise have a ferry on Platte. Met a train of mule packers from California. They left 16th of May, the same day that we crossed the Missouri. They say provision is cheap and plenty in California and the miners have done well. Passed many Indian wigwams which were erected near the Mormon establishment. Drove a considerable distance from the road to find grass, fuel and shelter from the wind, and find a good shelter and plenty of sage, but grass scant, and no water but alkali; however, we brought our cans full that will do us tonight. Saw snow on many of the peaks. Made 14 miles. The California train say they met the first emigration at Salt Lake, which is 250 miles from us.

June 29, Wednesday — This morning, and even the whole day, cold and windy. We all wear our winter clothing and suffer with cold at that. Betsey is considerable better today, and bore the jolting very well. The road has generally been smooth today, excepting two or three short and steep junctures. Came part of the day through heavy sand. Saw many dead cattle and several graves which we have noticed almost every day for many miles. We continue all day, near the Sweetwater and came several times to its banks. We took supplies from it and also watered the mules. It is the best water the country affords. Almost all other is considered poisonous. Our camp last night was near an alkali lake containing about 100 acres. Came 24 miles. Grass very scarce anywhere near the roads, being consumed by the numerous herds of cattle that pass through, and no doubt will be to the forks of the road. We had no scarcity until the roads all united. We camp in rather an incommodious place, both for fuel, water and grass.

Velina Williams headed to Oregon from Kanesville, Iowa on May 20, 1853. She reached the bridge crossing the North Platte on July 11 and Three Crossings on July 19. Her diary follows:

July 11 — About noon passed the bridge across Platte River, distant 55 miles from Fort Laramie. Learn that there is a new road by which we may avoid eight miles of desert. Camped about 1 o'clock in order that the cattle may have one-half day's rest today, that they may be better prepared for the 18-mile desert without feed or water.

July 12 — Found the road follows the Platte farther than we anticipated. Traveled all day over rough, hilly roads till we reached the point where the road leaves the river. We made our camp opposite the red bluffs. A creek which we called Skull Creek runs near.

July 13 — Remained in camp. Men went hunting, brought in antelope — a choice piece of meat.

(This camp, as I remember it, is the one where Brother Newell and myself came very near drowning. The creek is in the bottom of a ravine, the banks of which are some 12 or 15 feet high. The camp was just a little ways back from the bank and the creek was at that time a rather small, sluggish stream, rather crooked, and with deeper pools near the curves in the bank. Three of us, Cousin Alonzo, Newell and myself, thought it would be a good place to go in swimming, so we called it, though neither of us could swim. Accordingly we went down just below the camp and stripping off our clothes began splashing in the water that seldom reached above our knees. We kept following up stream, thinking we might find a pool waist deep in which we could splash around to better advantage. Just below the bank upon which the camp was pitched we found a large pool where the waters made an abrupt curve, having a considerable of a pond. Into this brother and I both waded, he at one side and I at the other. As the pond had two outlets, joining each other a short distance below, we soon found water waist deep, and throwing ourselves forward were prepared to go through swimming motions, while expecting to have the bottom of the pool safely within reach. Unfortunately there was a very deep hole there, quite beyond our depth. I went under, and when I tried to emerge found no bottom, and when my head did emerge I tried to call for help, but the water ran down my throat, strangling me, and under I went again. All this time I was striving to keep from sinking, and with the fear of drowning, I seemed to pass in review all my former life and wonder how the folks in the camp would feel when they found my body. I came out enough to see the tops of the wagon covers over the bank and to see my cousin sitting just under the top of the bank laughing at me. I struggled hard to cry out to him, but only succeeded in swallowing so much water that it seemed as though my lungs would burst. I had nearly given up struggling, and thinking that it was no use trying further, when O, joy, my hand came in contact with some grass at the edge of the pool and I came again into the light of day. I was so weak and exhausted that it was some little time before I could pull myself out on the bank, and when I did crawl out and was able to stand I found that my brother had got beyond his depth at nearly the same moment as myself and emerged at about the same time, while our cousin sitting up above the pool thought he was witnessing a strife between my brother and myself to see which could remain under the water the longer. I have read and heard many accounts of the painless feeling experienced by drowning persons, but my experience in Skull Creek convinced me that one can suffer ages of agony in the few moments preceding unconsciousness, and how much longer I have no desire to learn, by observation. — O. A. S.)

July 14 — Started early; passed Avenue Rocks. Here the

rocks form a gateway through which the road passes. High rock ridges present themselves on the right; those on the left are not so high. Passed Alkali Swamp; it is surrounded by high bluffs; a lot of alkali springs discharge their poison water into this reservoir; the water where it stands is black and smells bad; a whitish substance resembling saleratus is seen all around. Saw several buffalo. Found a convenient spot and camped early, as it is uncertain about finding grass again before we reach Sweetwater. Our men killed a buffalo today and we have a good supply of beef.

July 15 — Traveled four miles to a clear spring creek, thence three miles to Willow Springs, then passed over Prospect Hill, from the top of which we had a most beautiful view of the surrounding country. Halted on —— Creek to rest our cattle and eat our dinners. We then resumed our journey, not knowing that we should find anything for our cattle short of Sweetwater, 13 miles distant. Our captain and one or two others went off the road in different directions in search of grass; found a spot about two miles from where the road crosses Greasewood Creek; camped on the creek and drove the cattle to the grass. Traveled 17 miles.

July 16 — Crossed Greasewood and passed over sandy roads six miles to Saleratus Lake. The country all this distance is almost barren of anything except wild sage. The lake, or lakes, are in a valley almost entirely surrounded by high hills, which seem to be composed entirely of granite. The water, when disturbed, is black and smells bad; where it has evaporated there is white crust of saleratus; in some places it is quite pure, in others it is mixed with sand. Four miles from the lake we reached Independence Rock. This rock is a great curiosity. It stands in an open plain near Sweetwater, is 60 to 100 yards long, 100 or 150 wide, and probably 100 feet high, hard granite, lying on the top of the ground. Camped on Sweetwater, within sight of "Devil's Gate."

(As Aunt's diary is about complete as to the Platt River country, and that I may not forget to mention it later, I wish here to record an experience such as very few in crossing the plains ever witnessed and which no one hereafter will ever witness. This whole Platte region is subject to frequent, sudden and frightful thunderstorms. They come up and are generally accompanied or preceded by violent windstorms. The emigrants soon learned to prepare themselves to withstand these terrible storms and prevent the stampeding of their stock by placing their wagons in a circle, with the oxen on the inside, frequently chained to the wagon wheels by their heads. This method had the advantage not only of preventing loss of stock, but by concentrating in a small space all wagons offered more resistance to the wind and less surface to the storm. As the premonitory symptoms of a coming thunderstorm were usually the distant gathering of clouds on the horizon and the faint rumble of distant thunder, such sighs were sufficient warning to enable the trains to get ready to withstand their shock. While traveling one day on the Platte River, at some place, whose exact location I do not remember, a distant rumbling like thunder and a gathering cloud far to the south of west on the opposite side of the river caused the company to apprehend one of those storms, and the usual precautions were taken to meet it. Anxiously we watched the gathering cloud for the usual lightning flashes that accompanied such storms, but none were visible, and the cloud, while constantly growing in volume and rapidly nearing, seemed to be lighter in hue than usual with such storms. The noise of the thunder also seemed to be more continuous and while constantly increasing in volume, was not so intermittent as thunder usually was. The cloud, too, that at first seemed to be coming directly towards us was now seen to be following a course parallel to the river, and to follow the high, rolling tableland or bluffs on the south of the Platte. As the gathering cloud came nearer on the opposite side of the valley, some three or four miles, the ground seemed to fairly tremble, and one or two of the company who had crossed the plains several years before said that it was caused by an immense herd of buffalo. Soon the dust cloud was opposite us, when a gust of wind from down river lifted the cloud for awhile, and we beheld a compact black mass, extending beyond farther that we could see and coming in unbroken masses from the rear. The quaking of the earth and the rumble of the rushing torrent continued for a long time, many estimating the herd to be from four to eight miles long and of unknown width. Surely many, many thousands of those animals. Nothing even approximating it did we ever see before, nor did any of those with us who had crossed the plains before and who had seen many large herds previously. With this one exception, we saw but few buffalo while crossing the plains. Usually a small group of bulls or one or two solitary individuals, whose age and condition rendered them unfit for food. Antelopes were frequently seen, but these shy, fleet-footed creatures were seldom killed by any of our train, as we had very few hunters, and especially among the original members of our company but two guns. Before starting on our journey my father bought two rifles. One of these was a half-stock, smooth-bore gun which was turned over to Uncle Issacher Williams. The other was a long-barreled, full-stocked, steel rifle of about 32 to the pound calibre, that my father bought of Uncle George Cannon, who as an expert hunter and considered this rifle one of the best manufactured at that time. My Uncle Avery had two holster or "horse pistols," as they were called, and these, with the two rifles, constituted the entire armament of the Stearns families on that long, arduous, dangerous journey. The only time I ever knew of my father using his rifle was while coming up the Platte River. A number of large, white or buffalo wolves crossed our line of travel, and stopping our wagon, my father took out his rifle and ran across to the top of a sand ridge towards which the wolves were going and as they came opposite him shot one of them and dragged it down to the wagon. The wolf was not quite dead, the bullet having passed through his head at the junction of his jaw bones, cutting its tongue nearly off in its passage. It was a large, fierce-looking brute. There were also two kinds of grey wolves, one a small kind, somewhat near the size of the Western coyote, the other a larger one, but not quite as large as the buffalo wolf. Another feature of the country that she speaks about, the alkaline pools, that abound in that region. Emigrants learned to avoid turning their cattle loose near such places or allowing them to drink of the water, as it was nearly always fatal to them, as attested by the hundreds of dead cattle along the line of the road where these alkaline pools abound. Sometimes it seemed we were seldom out of reach of the stench of these dead animals, in all stages of decomposition. Many trains lost so many of their oxen from alkali poisoning that they had to abandon their wagons, having no oxen left to draw them. And yet the traders, who had their tents at intervals along the road, all claimed that cattle that were not over thirsty or jaded from travel could and did drink of these waters with impunity, which statement was verified by their having a large number of cattle grazing constantly in the immediate vicinity of these pools. These herds were almost always made up of cattle bought of emigrants, they having become too sorefooted to travel, or, as many shrewdly suspected, stolen from herds passing through the country by the Indians and turned over for goods to the traders, who were usually French Canadians, with Indian wives and half-breed families, and consequently on good terms with the Indians, with whom they associated and to whom they were connected by ties of kinship. — O. A. S.)

July 17 — This morning visited "Hells Gate" and found myself richly repaid for my walk of two and a half miles. It is a gorge in the rocks through which the Sweetwater forces its way. They are perpendicular and 400 feet high. The Wind River chain of the Rocky Mountains, along whose base we traveled, are literally made of rocks ranging from 1,200 to 1,500 and 2,000 feet high, and mostly bare of vegetation or earth. Traveled about 10 miles. Some snow on the mountains now at our left.

July 18 — Traveled about 17 miles over hilly roads. Camped on the Sweetwater; one of the cows missing tonight.

July 19 — Traveled 12 miles; crossed the Sweetwater three times. The road for two miles runs between rocky ridges, between which there is only room for the Sweetwater and the road.

On May 19, 1852 Enoch Conyers left Kanesville, Iowa, reached the upper ferry area on June 29, and the Three Crossings area on July 6. Included is a detailed description of his Independence Day celebration:

Our camp tonight is a few miles above the crossing of the North Platte, where the emigrants who traveled on the south side of the river crossed over to the road of those who traveled on the north side of the Platte. We understand that there is a bridge at this crossing of the Platte. Many of the emigrants crossed the Platte to the north side, just below Fort Laramie.

June 30 — Wednesday — We started at 10 a. m. and traveled over a very hard, rough road for sixteen miles and camped near a spring of clear water at the foot of the hill. The second spring quite swampy. Not much water for the cattle, but plenty of good, dry willow wood. Grass not good. Quite a number of cattle in our company are getting lame by traveling over hot, sandy and stony roads, but we very soon cure them up in the following manner: We cut a piece of hide from a dead ox by the roadside; making small holes in the border of this piece of hide; through these holes we run a string or a narrow strip of hide for a drawstring; we then put this piece of hide on the lame oxen's feet, flesh side out, drawing the string tight enough to hold it on the foot, and then tie it fast. This completes the job. Two days' wear is sufficient for a cure.

July 1 — Thursday. — We started at 7:45 a. m. and traveled about nine miles to a running stream of clear water. Here we stopped for lunch. After lunch we came twelve miles and camped on Sweetwater, on the east side of and near by the "Independence Rock." No wood to be had. We were obliged to drive our cattle seven miles, and then did not get very good grass. Hope we will get some soon, for our cattle stand in great need of some kind of feed, or we will soon be obliged to leave some of them by the roadside. Why this stream is called Sweetwater I know not, but after traveling over this road from the Missouri River to this stream, being obliged to drink alkali water or the roilly water from the River Platte, most all the way, it certainly causes this water to taste very sweet indeed; therefore the name, "Sweetwater," is quite appropriate.

July 2 — Friday. — Before starting on our way this morning the most of our company visited the summit of "Independence Rock." The trail leading to the summit is very narrow, and in some places quite dangerous, at times barely enough room for a foothold; but by steadying ourselves with our hands on the projecting rocks we succeeded in reaching the summit without any accident. From here we had a splendid view of the surrounding country for miles. We found the rock literally covered with the names of emigrants. We found some names that were recorded there in 1843. Some of these names were written with white or red chalk; some were cut in the rock with a cold chisel, whilst others were written with tar — and, in fact, were written in every conceivable manner. From the numerous names found written upon this rock, one would naturally suppose that every man, woman and child that ever passed this way had succeeded in writing or having their names written on this rock. We noticed a number of emigrants searching the rock for the names of relatives and friends who had passed this way in previous years, and the thought came to my mind: "How will it be in future years with emigrants traveling this way, who will be expecting to find the names of relatives and friends recorded upon this rock, and how sad their disapointment when finding the names of those loved ones carved with a pocketknife upon a small board placed at the head of some grave in a lonely spot by the roadside?" Independence Rock stands alone out on a level country, hence is peculiarity. Of course, all our names were added to the great multitude. Its name, as we understand it, was given by a party of emigrants who traveled this way many years ago, and celebrated the Fourth of July on the summit of this rock, and gave it the name of "Independence Rock." We started on our way at 7 a. m., came five and a quarter miles to the "Devil's Gate," which is something grand — perpendicular rocks of granite formation touring up 400 feet high on either side of the river, and the Sweetwater running between, having cut its way through this granite formation for about 1,000 feet in length, and about 130 feet in breadth. After passing through the Devil's Gate, poor old Dick — one of our oxen purchased in Missouri — passed in his checks. Here we met with a Frenchman by the name of Schambau, who, by the way, was with Colonel Fremont during his notable trip through this country in the '40s. About fifteen minutes before old Dick died, this man, Schambau, stepped up and inquired: "Who does that ox belong to?" On being informed that he belonged to Mr. Burns, he said: "Well, had I been here twenty minutes sooner I would have saved that ox for you. He has been alkalied." Then he added: "When I was with Fremont, we lost quite a number of our oxen before we discovered a remedy, but afterward we never lost a single head by poison or alkali." The following is the remedy he gave us: "Take one-half pint each of lard and syrup; warm just sufficient to mix good, and if the animal is bloated, add to this one-half pint of good vinegar and drench them immediately." This recipe proved a sovereign remedy, and we lost no more cattle.

Note. — This remedy I have tried after arriving in Oregon, on cattle that were poisoned by eating wild parsnip, and also larkspur, with the very best results, never having lost a single head on which this remedy was tried.

This man Schambau was building a trading post near the Devil's Gate with timber hauled from the mountains about six miles distant. He informed us that if we wished to lay over until after the 4th we would find plenty of good grass and water by driving away from the road about four miles south. After lunch, following his directions, we drove south about four miles, where we found the very best of grass, over knee high, and a creek of splendid, ice-cold water. Here we camped and intend staying until after the glorious 4th. This is a beautiful little valley, almost surrounded with mountains, with a rich, fertile soil, and room enough for four or five good farms. No sickness in our train now, the water having become too pure for that. Mr. Gay and family, formerly or Payson, Ill., joined our company today. He had been out to California, and now was returning overland with his family. He made the statement that he owned a farm near Oakland, Cal.

July 3 — Saturday. — We are now camped in a beautiful valley of the Sweetwater Mountains. Last night we permitted our cattle to feast on this good grass only for a few minutes at a time, for fear they would kill themselves if permitted to remain longer. We now can drink this good, cold mountain water to our hearts' content. It seems to give up a new lease of life. The nights are quite cool and chilly. Several of the boys started out this morning for a hunt in the mountains for the purpose of obtaining some fresh meat, if possible, for our Fourth of July dinner. Those who remain in camp are helping the ladies in preparing for the banquet. A number of wagon beds are being taken to pieces and formed into long tables. A little further on is a group of young ladies seated on the grass talking over the problem of manufacturing "Old Glory" to wave over our festivities. The question arose as to where we are to obtain the material for the flag. One lady brought forth a sheet. This gave the ladies an idea. Quick as thought another brought a skirt for the red stripes. Now we have the white and the red for the stripes, but where will we get the blue for the field? Another lady ran to her tent and brought forth a blue jacket, saying: "Here, take this; it will do for the field." Needles and thread were soon secured and the ladies went at their task with a will, one lady remarking that "Necessity is the mother of invention," and the answer came back, "Yes, and the ladies of our company are equal to the task." Some of the boys were gathering wood to cook the dinner, and others went after a liberty pole. In fact, every member of our company took hold with a willing hand to make our celebration on the plains a grand success. The boys who went out hunting early this morning returned to camp about 3 o'clock in the afternoon, some loaded with antelope, some with sagehens, and some with jackrabbits. Others brought a hugh snowball, inserting a pole through the center the easier to carry it. The game was quickly dressed and made ready for the cook, and the cooking was carried on to a late hour in the night. All being in readiness for the morrow, we retired to rest.

July 4 — Sunday. — The day was ushered in with the booming of small arms, which was the best that we could do under the circumstances, so far away from civilization. Although the noise was not so great as that made by cannon, yet it answered the purpose. Just before the sun made its appearance above the eastern horizon, we raised our forty-foot flagstaff with "Old Glory" nailed fast to the top, which waved as majestically and graceful as though it had been made of the best Japan silk. After the flagstaff was raised to its position our company circled around the old flag and sung "The Star Spangled Banner." Then three rousing cheers and a tiger were given to "Old Glory," The question came up, To whom should the honor be given to deliver the oration? This honor fell to the lot of Virgil Y. Ralston, a son of Dr. J. N. Ralston, of Quincy, Ill., and an old schoolmate of your humble servant. Unfortunately he, with several other young men of our company, went this morning to the Devil's Gate, where they obtained a little too much "firewater," and by the time they reached the camp were considerably under its influence. But this was the glorious old Fourth, therefore the oration we must have. The Declaration of Independence was read by R. L. Doyle, of Keokuk, Iowa, after which several of the boys gathered around Virgil, lifting him bodily upon the end of one of our long tables, where they steadied him until he became sufficiently braced up, and then let go of him. He spoke for over half an hour, and delivered, off-hand, an excellent oration. Just after the oration there came up a storm that threatened to spoil all our fun, but fortunately it lasted only a short time. All gathered around the tables loaded with refreshments, beautified and decorated with evergreens and wild flower of the valley, that speak volumes in behalf of the good taste displayed by the ladies, both in the decorative and culinary art. The following is our bill of fare in part:

MEATS

Roast Antelope, Roast Sagehen, Roast Rabbit, Antelope Stew, Sagehen Stew, Jack Rabbit Stew, Antelope Potpie, Sagehen Fried, Jack Rabbit Fried.

VEGETABLES

Irish Potatoes (brought from Illinois), Boston Baked Beans, Rice, Pickles.

BREAD

White Bread, Graham Bread, Warm Rolls, fresh from the oven.

PASTRY

Pound Cake, Fruit Cake, Jelly Cake, Sweetwater Mountain Cake, Peach Pie, Apple Pie, Strawberry Pie, Custard Pie. (A dozen or more varieties, both of cake and pies not enumerated.)

DRINKS

Coffee, Tea, Chocolate, and Good, Cold Mountain Water, fresh from the brook.

The snowball was brought into use in making a fine lot of Sweetwater Mountain ice cream.

No person left the table hungry. After our feast patriotic songs were indulged in, winding up with three cheers for Uncle Sam and three for Old Glory. Of course, the ladies were not forgotten, and three rousing cheers were given for them. Take it altogther, we passed an enjoyable day — a Fourth of July on the plains never to be forgotten.

July 5 — Monday. — We started on our way at 6:30 a. m. Leaving Old Glory nailed fast to the masthead; with three rousing cheers to the old flag, we again started on our way to the setting sun. Our cattle, being refreshed by their rest, started off quite brisk. At about 11 a. m. we passed the camp where on Saturday, July 3, some emigrants hung a man for murder. We did not learn the names. The company chose a judge to preside over the trial, and a sheriff, who empaneled a trial jury of twelve men, who heard all the evidence, after which the judge charged the jury. The jury retired a short distance from camp, under the charge of the sheriff chosen by the company for the emergency, for their deliberation. In about twenty minutes they returned and informed the court that they had decided on a verdict. The foreman then handed their written verdict to the court, which read as follows: "We, the jury, do find the defendant guilty of murder in the first degree, as charged." Signed by all the jurors. The court immediately passed sentence on the defendant, to be hanged by the neck until dead, dead, dead, and may God have mercy on your soul. The company ran two wagons together, elevating the tongues in the shape of the letter "A," tying them together. On this improvised gallows the defendant was hung until life was pronounced extinct. Near by two graves were dug, one for the murdered man, the other for the murderer. Their burial being completed, the company started on their way. We traveled twenty-two miles today over a heavy, sandy road, and camped on Sweetwater. No wood and grass very scarce.

July 6 — Tuesday. — We started at 6:30 a. m. About noon we passed a train that had stopped for lunch by the roadside. Just as we came abreast of them we observed three men seated on the tongue of one of their wagons, when a large-sized woman, weighing something over 250 pounds, with sleeves rolled up above her elbows, stepped out in front of the three men, smacking her fists and shaking them under the nose of the little man seated in the center, as though she intended to leave nothing but a greast spot after she got through with him. Then she commenced a harangue of abusive language that ought to shame the most profane person on the face of the earth. This little man she dominated was her husband. She berated him for everything that was good, bad, or indifferent, charging him with bringing his wife and children out into this God-forsaken country to starve and die. To the honor of the little man, I will say, that he sat there like a bump on a log, seemingly taking it all good-naturedly, without making any answer whatever. Perhaps he was afraid to open his mouth in self-defense, and that silence was the better part of valor. This much I have learned since we started across the continent. That if there is anything in this world that will bring to the surface a man's bad traits, it is a trip across the continent with an ox team. In honor and justice to our little family, I must say that we have thus far gotten along together splendidly, without any display whatever, more especially such scenes as we have witnessed by the roadside today. And the school of experience which we are daily passing through, witnessing scenes so repulsive and disgusting, would almost drive one to believe that the whole human race, with but few exceptions, were hypocrites. We traveled twenty miles today, and camped on the Sweetwater. We crossed this stream three times today. The last two crossings were the worst, on account of the rock or boulders that were in the river. Grazing is very poor, and no wood tonight. William has been very sick all day. We had quite a hard frost this morning.

Part III
A Pictorial Journey Back
In Time

About the Artists

MOST OF THE paintings and drawings that follow in the book are the works of William Henry Jackson, Alfred J. Miller, and William Henry Tappan, who accompanied Osborne Cross.

Jackson was born in 1843, the third year of the Oregon Trail's use by the emigrants. By the time he followed the trail west in 1866, it had meandered some from its early starting point of Independence, Missouri. In 1866 Jackson signed on as a bullwhacker for an ox team freight wagon train and headed for California along most of the Oregon Trail. It was during this time that he made many of the sketches that later became the basis for his paintings which appear here.

By 1869 his interests centered in photography, and his photographic diary of the opening of the West is well-known. He became the official photographer of the Hayden Survey of the territories and took the first photos of the Yellowstone area. Perhaps the finest exhibition of his Oregon Trail works is on permanent display at Scotts Bluff National Monument, under the direction of the National Park Service. His interest and work in the West continued until he died in 1942. Many of his paintings based on his early sketches were done in the early 1930s. Unless noted otherwise, the paintings labeled National Park Service may be found in the Oregon Trail Museum at the national monument. Another location for many of his works is the Pioneer Museum in Minden, Nebraska.

Osborne Cross served as a major in the U.S. Army. In

1849 the government ordered Col. W. W. Loring to head west with a regiment of mounted riflemen and to leave detachments of troops at the newly-established Fort Kearny and newly purchased Fort Laramie, to establish a post in the vicinity of Fort Hall, and finally proceed to Fort Vancouver. Maj. Osborne Cross served as the acting quartermaster and was responsible for making an accurate and detailed report of their march west. The drawings included helped to chronicle the march. They are taken from his report and the book, *The March of the Mounted Riflemen.* While the drawings that illustrate the book were not signed, Raymond Settle holds that they were done by William Henry Tappan. Tappan had asked permission to accompany the Mounted Riflemen on their journey to "make such drawings and collections as will illustrate the geological features, the zoological and botanical products of the country." He was granted permission, and thus it seems reasonable to assume that he made them. Other people, however, have thought that the drawings might have been done by George Gibbs, another artist on the journey to Oregon.

Alfred Jacob Miller (1810–1873) was a Baltimore painter who was hired by Sir William Drummond Stewart, a Scottish patrician, to accompany him on his journey to the West and the Rocky Mountains. His only duty was to "sketch the remarkable scenery and incidents of the journey." With William Sublette as their guide, they left St. Louis, Missouri, in May and headed west along part of the route that later was to become the Oregon Trail; along the Platte, through the South Pass and the Green River area to the rendezvous. Here Miller set about his work in earnest. Altogether, he made one hundred sixty-six sketches which were used as the basis for his oil paintings. His works are some of the few firsthand pictorial records of the scenic wonders, Indians, and mountain men that inhabited the West in 1837.

Pictorial Section

As part of the preparation for this publication, the author studied many of the early sketches, drawings, and photographs made along the trail. The exact locations from which the early drawings were made were sought out, and then corresponding photographs were taken. When the exact locations could not be identified or if they were not accessible, approximate locations were chosen as close as possible to the original. By comparing the present-day photographs with the earlier items, one notices immediately the accuracy of most of the early works. But like most artists, sometimes their views were romanticized or idealized. This, however, does not diminish their reality, but perhaps reflects the awe and excitement of the artists at such grand sights.

The description of the emigrant wagon is taken from Randoph Marcy's *The Prairie Traveler.*

Below is part of an interpretive display on the mode of transportation used by the early emigrants.

— *Solomon D. Butcher Collection, Nebraska State Historical Society*

This is an early photo of an emigrant family going west. While this shows horses, oxen were more durable and less likely to be stolen by Indians.

Mode of transportation used by the author on his various treks west. It was complete with two spares, front and back, gas can, extra water and three planks for use in crossings or if stuck in "soft spots."

Here is part of an interpretive display showing the supplies and clothing required by an emigrant as taken from Joseph Ware's *The Emigrant Guide to California*.

— Western History Department, Denver Public Library

Emigrants at rest on their trek west.

— National Archives

Inside of an emigrant wagon shows items taken from their home. Unfortunately, they were frequently forced to jettison many of their beloved items along the trail to lighten the loads. In places, the trail was littered with goods and even food.

One of the early morning tasks for emigrants was to get their oxen yoked up. Here they are being readied at Rock Creek Station.

The buffalo were one of the sights that thrilled the emigrants. The thunder and dust of the great herds awed many pioneers. Today they are often found in zoos, as is this one in Ross Park, Pocatello, Idaho.

Antelope were frequently seen and hunted by the emigrants. Today they still roam in many areas mentioned in diaries. These were seen just north of Twin Buttes.

The rattlesnake was one of the creatures encountered along the trail. There are accounts of emigrants dying from a snake bite, and they certainly are not to be played with. This one was encountered east of Independence Rock.

The Oregon Trail and the land were hard on the emigrants and their animals. Even today, ranches lose stock, as is evident right next to the trail. James Wilkins, traveling this very section along the Sweetwater, noted "dead oxen lay on the road. today nearly every hundred yards, the nausious effluria arising from so much putrid flesh, was offensive to the extreme."

Death was a constant companion some years on the trail. This is the grave of Susan O. Hail in the Sand Hills near the Platte River in Nebraska.

— *Western History Collection, Natural History Museum of Los Angeles County*

Indian camps were encountered by the emigrants. Here is an early photograph of one. A similar scene today is shown of a camp being set up for a tribal celebration.

Wagon breakdowns happened often and sometimes had to be abandoned. This is part of an interpretive display at Three Island Crossing, Idaho.

This wagon can be found at the new Rock Creek Station Park in Nebraska. Behind it is the deep swale of the trail as it came up the hill from Rock Creek.

Another of the many graves still found along the trail. Few graves have been identified. Many were dug up by wolves and coyotes after emigrants finished burying their dead and moved on. Sometimes they were buried right in the trail in hopes that the animals would not find them.

Here is a trapper's tipi which serves as part of the living display at Fort Laramie, Wyoming.

William Henry Jackson's impression of what Westport Landing might have looked like during the 1840s depicts a bustling scene. The photo below shows the same area today.

The first "temporary" courthouse of Independence, Missouri, built in 1827, still stands today.

This is Spring Park near Courthouse Square, Independence. The restored cabin is the Brady or Younger cabin. It was built about 1836.

— Kansas State Historical Society

Courthouse Square, Independence, Missouri, as it appeared to the emigrants in the late 1850s.

A modern courthouse now stands at Independence. Inside are remnants of the earlier courthouse foundations.

This is the West Building of the Shawnee Methodist Mission constructed in 1839.
It is open to visitors and is run by the Kansas Historical Society.

A sandstone building is part of the original St. Mary's Catholic Potawatomie Mission
established when the Catholic missionaries came to Christianize the Indians in 1848.

— *National Park Service*

A painting of Alcove Spring by William Henry Jackson. The spring was named by Edwin Bryant in 1846, and it is east of the Independence Ford of the Big Blue River in Kansas. Below, Alcove Spring as seen today. Due to vandalism in the area, it is closed to the public and is nearly impossible to locate unless you know the area. This photo was taken in August. The emigrants would have been here in early May when there would be more water. The spring is behind the bushes at the right.

The original Hollenberg ranch house constructed in 1859 sits just west of the junction of the St. Jo and Independence roads of the Oregon Trail. Little is different at the house, but irrigation and farming have changed the land surrounding it.

— *California State Library*

This early ambrotype of Rock Creek Station was taken about 1859. The Oregon Trail forded Rock Creek here until David McCanles built the East Ranch and bridge in 1859. Some people think the horseman on the right is McCanles. In 1861 the East Ranch became the setting for the "famous" Hickok-M'Kanlas Gang shootout of the "Dime Novels" which helped to make Hickok famous. The real truth was much less romantic, with Hickok more of a villain than hero. The present photo below is made from about the same spot. Note the location of the well in both photos. The clearing in the center background is the Oregon Trail heading past the West Ranch. Reconstruction of the ranch buildings is presently under way. The slab foundations for the East Ranch buildings are visible.

— National Park Service

Here is Jackson's painting of the crossing of Rock Creek, with the wagon pulling up the west hill. Some people feel he based this painting on the earlier reverse image of the East Ranch. (See previous page.)

This photograph looks back at the crossing. Note the wagon team that is part of the present living display at Rock Creek, Nebraska, also the foundation (right) for reconstruction of the ranch buildings.

Jackson's view of the Sand Hills of Nebraska, along the Platte River Valley. Below is a photo of a similar area today.

Jackson's painting of Fort Kearny, Nebraska. Note the cottonwood trees in the painting. They were planted by Lt. Daniel P. Woodbury when the fort was constructed. Some of the original trees may still be seen standing in the photo below, surrounding the parade ground. Today new trees are replanted as the old ones die.

Ruts are clear as the Oregon Trail is about to plunge down Windlass Hill into Ash Hollow. Further down, the eroded scars are evident.

Looking back up Windlass Hill, the different routes of the trail down the hill stand out on the grade.

One of the major landmarks along the Platte River Valley was Courthouse and Jail Rock. Above is James Wilkins' drawing, and below a photo of the same area. The rocks were off the main branch of the trail, and many emigrants took side trips to see and climb on them. The modern "emigrant" may do the same. The first written appearance of the name "Court House" was by A. J. Miller in 1837, and "Jail" by John Kerns in 1852.

— Courtesy A. T. Esles, Sotheby & Co., London, and Robert Warner's
"The Fort Laramie of Alfred Jacob Miller"

Alfred Miller passed "Court House" Rock on his journey west. Here is his drawing of the area. His notation: "Curious formation of Earth Near the Platte River." Below is a photo of the same area, but today the Indians are gone.

Here are Jackson's pencil sketches of Chimney Rock and the Platte Valley, and Castle and Table Rock. Notice how accurate was his sketch of Castle and Table Rock. You can almost feel being with Jackson when he made his sketch, as photograph below shows.

— National Park Service

Here is the famous Jackson painting of Chimney Rock and the Platte River Valley.
Below is a photo from a similar spot off the modern highway.

— *Walters Art Gallery, Baltimore*

This is how Alfred J. Miller saw Chimney Rock in 1837, and as it appears today. The chimney has lost much of its height in the past century and a half. The first recorded use of the name "Chimney" was in Joshus Pilcher's report in 1827.

Chimney Rock was one of the most eyecatching landmarks along the trail. Many drawings were made, and it seems most emigrants mentioned it in their diaries. This is Jackson's painting and a modern photo.

Here is Frederick Piercy's view of Chimney Rock from 1855, and a similar view taken from near the display area off the highway.

— *National Park Service*

Henry Jackson's drawing of campground, and a similar photo taken of the living display at Scotts Bluff.

— *Walters Art Gallery, Baltimore*

Alfred Miller's romantic painting of the area now known as Scotts Bluff. The modern photo shows man's encroachment both from agriculture and technology.

Here is famous Mitchell Pass at Scotts Bluff. Jackson passed through the area and camped there in 1866. Below is a photo of the same area today. Note the Oregon Trail curves across the photo near the bottom. Visitors may walk the trail here.

— National Park Service

Jackson painted this view west of Mitchell Pass, looking back. Fort Mitchell is shown, but it was occupied only from 1864–67. Nothing is left of Fort Mitchell today. This photo was taken beside an historical marker, but the fort's location was about a mile farther down the road to the left.

Alfred Miller visited Fort William (Fort Laramie) in 1837. Here are his paintings of the outside and inside of the fort. It was replaced by Fort John in 1841. Nothing remains of Fort William, and historians disagree as to the specific location, but they all agree it was near the present Fort Laramie. These are part of the displays at Fort Laramie today.

This is the earliest photo of Fort Laramie, taken in 1858. At left is the old adobe
Fort John, constructed in 1841. Also evident is Old Bedlam. Below is a photo taken
from about the same place. Fort John is no more. Note how the trees obscure the
location of the fort and river today.

This display at Fort Laramie shows the Sutler's store in 1877. Below is a recent photo, showing a similar scene.

Above photograph shows the burial place of Mini Aku, daughter of the Sioux Chief Spotted Tail. She died in 1866. Fort Laramie is in the background. This was the same year Jackson came to Fort Laramie. Below is a view of the same locale today.

The Oregon Trail Ruts Display, near Guernsey, Wyoming, preserves for future generations a sampling of how the trail actually appeared, sans Hollywood's interpretation. Clayton's guidebook notes: "Steep hill to ascend and descend . . . you will find the road rocky in places, and about half way over there is sudden turn in the road over rough rocks, which is dangerous to wagons, if care is not taken." Shown is start of the ascent and some of those "rough rocks."

— National Park Service

Jackson's version of Laramie Peak and the approach to La Bonte Creek are seen in this top photograph. Below is a view taken from the trail as it nears La Bonte Creek today, far different from the earlier painting.

— Original painting, Harold Warp, Pioneer Village, Minden, Nebraska

Fort Caspar and the Platte River Bridge as painted by Jackson. Emigrants traveling the south side of the Platte crossed to the north side between Deer Creek at Glenrock and the Red Buttes at Bessemer Bend. Fort Caspar was only one of many crossing areas. Note the existence of trees and the partial reconstruction of the bridge in the photo.

— Fort Casper Museum. Wyoming

The famous Red Buttes at Bessemer Bend were photographed by Jackson in 1870. The emigrants crossed the North Platte at this ford, only they crossed from the far side of the river. The ford was used by most emigrants prior to 1847 and after that by those who did not want to or could not pay the tolls for the bridge or ferries at Casper. A recent photo (below) taken from the same historic place shows a bridge over the North Platte, the growth of trees, and a ranch fence. A small park and interpretive display are in the area located at the bend of the river at the far right.

— Original painting. Harold Warp. Pioneer Village. Minden. Nebraska

This painting of the Red Buttes was also done by Jackson. The creek more visible here is the Poison Spider. By the late 1840s, variants of the trail were on both sides of the river at this last fording area of the North Platte. The lower view was taken from the swales of the trail looking down into what Clayton's guide calls "Rock Avenue and steep descent" on the route from the crossing of the North Platte to the Sweetwater River.

Rock Avenue in closeup near the bottom. Horn's guidebook changed the name to "Avenue Rock," noting "the rocks here form a gateway through which the road passes; several rocky ridges present themselves on the right." The present road has obliterated much of the trail in this area.

Part of the famous "Willow Springs" is today covered by an old spring house. This was a major resting and camping area on the trail crossing over to the Sweetwater from the North Platte.

— Original painting. Harold Warp. Pioneer Village. Minden. Nebraska. and National Park Service

Jackson captured Independence Rock, along the Sweetwater River, on canvas in such views as these. He showed the approach to the famous promontory through eyes of the emigrants. The modern highway traveler comes upon the rock from a different

angle. For comparison, a recent photograph indicates how it appears today. Like many early frontier painters, Jackson exaggerated and dramatized at times to gain effect. Here, he shows a large "Devil's Gate" in the background, yet in reality it is barely visible.

William Henry Tappan sketeched Independence Rock in 1849. The whole area surrounding the rock was a campground. Emigrants forded the Sweetwater from a point immediately west of the rock to just about a mile from Devil's Gate. Today the buffalo are gone, but cattle and antelope roam in the area (below).

— Original painting, Harold Warp, Pioneer Village, Minden, Nebraska

This view of Independence Rock painted by Jackson shows why it came to be called the "Great Registry of the Desert." In 1852 E. W. Conyers ". . . found the rock literally covered with the names of emigrants . . . written with white or red chalk . . . cut in the rock with a cold chisel . . . others written with tar and, in fact, were written in every conceivable manner." He had also found some names from 1843. The photo below shows a comparable view with the land contour much the same. Note the change, however, in the river channel.

Devil's Gate viewed from the east by William Henry Tappan near the last fording place. The recent photo of the same area shows the Dumbell Ranch that now occupies the location of the ford.

J. Goldsborough Bruff made this drawing in 1849. It shows the pass the emigrants used near Devil's Gate. A modern highway now bypasses it; the older highway, however, follows the trail through the pass.

— Original painting, Harold Warp, Pioneer Village, Minden, Nebraska

Devil's Gate as viewed by Jackson from the west along the trail. The old highway follows the Oregon Trail. Devil's Gate measures about 370 feet deep and 1,500 feet long and varying in width, with 50 feet at its narrowest point. The modern traveler can observe it from a newly-built vantage point on the hill overlooking the area.

— National Park Service

Split Rock served as a landmark for the emigrants after passing Devil's Gate. Above is Jackson's painting to compare with the photo below. Miller made one of the earliest sketches of this area in 1837.

This is the approach to the Three Crossing of the Sweetwater. Some emigrants bypassed it by taking the Deep Sand route away from the river. Others forded the river three times within a mile and a half, because of the narrow gorge. It can be seen in the distance. The painting above is Jackson's.

St. Mary's Station was painted by Jackson. The current photo was taken past the actual location, but in the near vicinity. The trail cuts over the large hill, right of center, in the background.

Notorious Rocky Ridge which the trail traversed looks like this. William Clayton's emigrant guide noted "Rough, rocky, ridges — dangerous to wagons, and ought to be crossed with care." It is no less true today. Even a modern 4 x 4 had trouble negotiating the rocks. Walking is much safer. It is easy to get caught on some of those rocks. Wagons had much higher ground clearance.

— Original painting, Harold Warp, Pioneer Village, Minden, Nebraska

Burnt Ranch and the last or ninth crossing of the Sweetwater River since it was first encountered before Independence Rock. The starting point for the Lander Road was also here. The painting is Jackson's.

— National Park Service

Jackson's pencil drawing of Twin Mounds shows a landmark on the trail as it approaches South Pass. The drawing shows the freighters hunting antelope which may still be found in the area, seen in this present-day view.

— Original painting, Harold Warp, Pioneer Village, Minden, Nebraska

Here are the Wind River Mountains and the trail on its approach to the Dry Sandy
Crossing. For the emigrants it was about one day west of the great South Pass. This
has often been designated as the South Pass. The photo is taken from the swales left
of the emigrant wagons as they approached the Dry Sandy.

Haystack Butte was sketched by Bruff in 1849. This was a minor landmark on the Sublette Cutoff. If Bruff were alive today he might think it was still 1849.

This painting is from Ghent's *The Road to Oregon* and shows the emigrants being ferried across the Green River. The photo below is from the location of the Case Ferry where the Baker-Davis Cutoff crosses the Green to join with the Slate Creek Cutoff. This cutoff later intercepts the Sublette Cutoff. The artist "enlarged" the mountains in the background. Today, there is a camping area where the emigrants would have landed after crossing. The river is not as wide due to a dam just upriver to control its flow.

— *National Park Service*

Jackson's painting of the Mormon handcarts and a recent photo of some Mormon students reliving a page in their history.

Fort Bridger as shown in Stansbury's *An Expedition to the Valley of the Great Salt Lake of Utah* (1852). Fort Bridger appears like this today, with Bridger Butte in the background. It is now an historic site.

— State Historical Society of Wisconsin

James Wilkins drew this sketch showing the descent of the Bear River Mountains. He described it as ". . . ascend and descend the mountain the steepest and longest ascent . . . the government wagons (part of the Regiment of Mounted Riflemen) following close behind. I made a sketch of the descent on the other side, but owing to the clouds of dust, it was anything but pleasant to sit sketching." Today the scars are evident where they came down the mountain just east of Dingle Station, as seen in the photo below.

Osborne Cross visited Fort Hall in 1849, and William Henry Tappan made these drawings of the outside and the inside buildings.

Here is the reproduction of Fort Hall south of Pocatello at Ross Park. Much research went into the project of reconstructing the replica. It looks as though Cross would feel "at home" here.

— National Park Service

Three Island Crossing was a major ford of the Snake River. The origin of the name is obvious. Some emigrants did not ford the Snake, but stayed on the southern bank meeting the northern route again at the ford near Fort Boise. Today the town of Glenns Ferry is located at Three Island Crossing. The painting is Jackson's, and a recent photo shows a similar view.

Here is Tappan's drawing of the bluffs along the Snake River on the southern alternate. Emigrants were often "forced" to remain on the south side when the Snake was too high and dangerous to ford at Three Island Crossing. Such was the case for the Mounted Riflemen. Below is the photo of the bluff where the Oregon Trail returns to the Snake a few miles southeast of Walter's Ferry, after cutting across Sinker Creek Flats.

Here is another of Tappan's drawings made along the southern alternate route. Below is a photo of the same promontory today, known as Lizard Butte, taken one mile southeast of Marsing, Idaho.

Nothing remains today of old Fort Boise. This is Tappan's exterior view of the fort. He also made an interior sketch. Below is a replica of Fort Boise that is being built in a park in Parma, about five miles southeast of its original location.

The modern highway heads up a small valley towards the Keeney Pass. The trail is to the left of the highway, as the swales show clearly.

Farewell Bend was the emigrants' last view of the Snake after having followed it for nearly 350 miles. Now they left the Snake, heading for the Blue Mountains.

— *National Park Service*

Jackson's painting of the emigrants' descent of the Ladd Canyon Hill into the Grand Ronde shows the trail coming down the side into the canyon. The trail ran actually more along the ridges and then cut diagonally across the face, as shown in Tappan's sketch (see following). Jackson's route is somewhat similar to a later stage route. Below is a photo from the general vicinity in a clearing made by the pipeline. Today a highway rest stop is nearby.

William Henry Tappan drew the descent into the Grande Ronde from the bottom, looking back up. This is more accurate than Jackson's. It is taken from the rest area off the highway.

— Original painting, Harold Warp, Pioneer Village, Minden, Nebraska

In the notorious Blue Mountains, emigrants feared getting bogged down by early winter snows. Jackson's painting shows ruggedness of the mountains. Driving the modern highway, you tend to lose much of the feeling of the trail.

Descent from the Blue Mountains was depicted by Tappan. Within a few miles, the emigrants had traveled from the cool forest in the mountains to the hot, dry sage-covered plains. The photo below shows traces of the trail, but mainly, pipelines and ranch roads now come down the hill.

The Whitman Mission had been burned long before Jackson made a painting of it; however, his painting is quite accurate except for the roof lines. Perhaps he used a drawing made later by one of the children who survived the massacre. The current photo shows reconstruction of the site.

This is Jackson's Barlow Road as it crosses the Cascade Mountains and approaches Mount Hood. It seems, however, that this may have been made from a location other than the Barlow Road. Below is a photo taken off the Barlow Road at Summit Meadows.

— #791, *Oregon Historical Society*

Here is the "end of the trail" — Oregon City as it appeared in 1848 and was painted
by Sir Henry Warre. The photograph below shows the city in 1857. Note that they
are views from opposite ends of the town. It was taken by Lorenzo Lorrain.

— #21079 *Oregon Historical Society*

Oregon City as seen today from similar viewpoints. The location of the mills made it difficult to find the spot used by Sir Henry Warre, but it is close. Downtown Oregon City has changed, but the background is similar in the photo below to Lorrain's photo.

— *Yale University, Beinecke Rare Book and Manuscript Library*

The other "end of the trail" was Fort Vancouver on the banks of the Columbia. This painting was made about 1845 by Paul Kane. The artist worked near where the present visitor center is located. The photo below was taken from near the same location.

— Fort Vancouver National Historic Site

Dr. John McLoughlin, sometimes called "the Father of Oregon," was the Chief Factor of the Hudson's Bay Company at Fort Vancouver. He did more to help the American emigrants to Oregon that any other single person. Yet in doing so, he was frequently criticized by the company. After Oregon officially became part of the United States, he was treated poorly by the government and many of the later emigrants. When he died in 1857, he had lost much of his property and was nearly penniless. This is perhaps one of the greatest tragedies of the Oregon experience.

— *Western History Department, Denver Public Library*

Recent scholarly research by William Welling contends that this photograph of Kit Carson (standing) has often been incorrectly labeled as including John C. Fremont. The man seated is not Fremont, but Edwin Perin. Fremont's picture follows. Kit Carson served as guide for Fremont on his expeditions west.

John C. Fremont was called the "pathfinder." He led expeditions to the Rockies, Oregon, and California in 1842, 1842–43, and 1844–45. The reports to Congress and subsequent publications brought Fremont, Carson, and Oregon to public attention.

— #3445, *Oregon Historical Society*

Samuel Kimborough Barlow, along with Philip Foster, was the developer of the Mount Hood Road, a wagon road better known as the Barlow Road, from "the dalls Mission to Valey of Clackamus."

— Kansas Historical Society

Jim Bridger — famous mountain man, guide, fur trader, and businessman — helped open the West to the emigrants. He started working for William Ashley in the Rocky Mountains in 1822 and continued as a guide into the 1860s. He claimed to be the discoverer of the Great Salt Lake, and many places were named for him. He was one of the last of the early mountain men to die, July 17, 1881, on his farm outside Independence, Missouri, near where the Oregon Trail began.

— National Park Service, Whitman Mission National Historic Site

Narcissa and Marcus Whitman set up their mission at Waiilatpu. Their hospitality was well-known to the early emigrants.

Rev. Jason Lee, a Methodist missionary, went west in 1834 and established a mission in the upper Willamette Valley. His relative, David Lee, later set up a mission at The Dalles in 1838.

— #8342, Oregon Historical Society

Father Pierre DeSmet, a Jesuit missionary, went west in 1840. He became one of the most influential missionaries in the West.

— Library of Congress

Part IV
Blaze Marks Along the Route

Major Museums and Displays

Jefferson National Expansion Memorial,
St. Louis, Missouri —

This is located on the site of the original settlement of St. Louis. On the grounds is the Gateway Arch commemorating the westward trek — "Gateway to the West." Within the visitor center under the arch is the Museum of Westward Expansion. This is one of the finest museums covering the whole period of westward migration, including the Oregon Trail. Inside are film shows and many exhibits starting with Jefferson and the Lewis and Clark expedition, the fur trade and mountain men, the Oregon and California emigrants, the Indians, the cowboys, the homesteaders, the railroads, and the closing of the West. Inside the display areas, park personnel talk about the different displays. This is the place to begin, and be sure you spend a few hours looking and listening. The park is located on the Mississippi River near the junction of I-55 and I-70 in downtown St. Louis.

Independence, Missouri and the Kansas City Vicinity —

Within this general area can be found numerous sites, displays, and museums. Included would be the courthouse and Courthouse Square, considered the starting point of the Oregon Trail; the Emigrant Spring which helped to make Independence famous, and the Brady cabin moved to the site in the past few years. The Wornall Home built in 1858 is open to the public, as is the cabin at the spring. Another house in the area is that of Col. Jack

Harris which was constructed about 1855. Jim Bridger's grave is in the Mount Washington Cemetery. Also in the area is the Shawnee Methodist Mission. Three buildings stand from the 1839–45 period. They have been restored and are open to the public. Many emigrants stopped here before their plunge onto the Central Plains. The Kansas State Historical Society is responsible for the museum.

Hollenberg Ranch, Hanover, Kansas —

This ranch was built in 1857 near the junction of the Independence and St. Jo Roads. The building is still on its original site. Inside is a small museum and display area devoted primarily to its role during the Pony Express era. To the Oregon emigrants, it was the Cottonwood Station. It is located about one mile east of Hanover on Kansas 243.

Rock Creek Station, Nebraska —

At this time, there is only a small display and park, but an immense amount of work is being done under the direction of Wayne Brandt, the park superintendent. While this was not a major site during the early Oregon Trail's history, it did play a large part in the history of the area. McCanles built a toll bridge over Rock Creek and ranch here in 1859. It also became the site of the infamous Hickok-McCanles fight. It is the archeological work, much of which is now completed and the plans for reconstruction that make this site worthy of the time it would take. Plans also include an area for camping and picnics. Located about seven miles east of Fairbury off Nebraska 8, is under the jurisdiction of the Nebraska Game and Parks Commission.

Fort Kearny, Nebraska —

Today this is a State Historic Site and in the visitor center is a museum which tells the story of the fort's development.

A film center deals with its reconstruction and history. Buildings reconstructed include the blacksmith shop, stockade, and a recently-collapsed powder magazine. As mentioned earlier, some of the trees planted by Lieutenant Woodbury in 1848 around the parade grounds are still alive. It is located south and east of Kearny just west of Nebraska 10.

Ash Hollow, Nebraska —

Here are fine examples of trail ruts down Windlass Hill, the Ash Hollow Spring, the cemetery, a campground where the emigrants camped, and a fine visitor center. In the visitor center is a good museum and displays covering the entire history of Ash Hollow, including the Oregon period. Unfortunately, vandalism has occurred to some of the displays. It is located on U.S. 26 as it approaches the North Platte from the south.

Courthouse and Jail Rock and
Chimney Rock, Nebraska —

These were some of the major landmarks on the Oregon Trail. Mobile museums have been set up at each telling the history and records of emigrants reactions to these sights are included. Both are in the vicinity of Bridgeport, Nebraska off highway 92. Courthouse and Jail Rock are about five miles south, while Chimney Rock is fifteen miles west.

Scotts Bluff, Nebraska —

Here is famous Mitchell Pass and the Oregon Trail Museum with its living display. You can still walk along the Oregon Trail through the pass, just as the emigrants did years ago. Within the visitors center are many exhibits about the history of the area, including Robidoux Pass. This is also the location of many of the original William Henry Jackson sketches and paintings. A scenic drive can also take you to the top of Scotts Bluff. Some of the early emigrants did the same thing, only they had to climb it. It is located on highway 92 just outside Gering.

Fort Laramie, Wyoming —

The fort contains many of the old buildings restored from the military period after 1848, including Old Bedlam, the Sutlers Store, officers quarters, the guard house, bakery, barracks, and many others. Its living displays and museum make it one of the best on the trail and the pride and joy of the Park Service. For the emigrants, it was a high point of their travel, as it is for the modern traveler today. It is well worth the few hours it takes to walk the grounds. Depending on the day visited, you can talk to the sutler, infantryman, cavalry people, bakers, traders, wives of enlisted men and officers. It is located three miles west of the town of Fort Laramie, off highway U.S. 26.

Oregon Trail Ruts and Register Cliff, Wyoming —

Here is vivid physical evidence of the emigrants' trek west. The wagon wheels cut their way through the rocks on the hills in the area. In some places, the ruts are cut over three feet in depth into the rocks. Here also, the emigrants carved their names into Register Cliff and buried their dead along side the trail. They are located south of Guernsey off of U.S. 26.

Fort Caspar, Wyoming —

Today the fort has been reconstructed to its original appearance and houses a fine museum and displays. Outside you can see a partial reconstruction of the Platte River Bridge. Additional materials are on display in the museum which has recently been opened. The fort is located in the western part of Casper on Fort Caspar Road.

Independence Rock, Wyoming —

This is one of the most famous landmarks on the Oregon Trail. It has been called "the Great Registry of the Desert," because of the emigrants' practice of carving their names on it. There is a small interpretive display in the area, and one can climb it as many emigrants did years ago. It is located on Wyoming highway 220 about fifty miles southwest of Casper.

South Pass, Wyoming —

This is the gentle saddle through which the emigrant trains rolled and where the Oregon Territory began. There is a small interpretive display west of the pass. Unfortunately, it has been the subject of much vandalism. At the actual South Pass are two trail markers. One was placed by Ezra Meeker in 1906 when he retraced his oxen trip to Oregon. The other was placed in honor of Narcissa Whitman and Eliza Spalding, the first Caucasian women to use South Pass. The display is located on Wyoming 28 about forty-five miles southwest of Lander.

Fort Bridger, Wyoming —

A State Historic Site and a living museum, this famous fort has displays from the trading period through its military period. The surviving buildings are all from the military era after 1858. Those restored are the barracks, commander and officers quarters, guardhouse, and the sutler's complex. It is located off I-80 on U.S. 30 in the town of Fort Bridger.

Fort Hall, Idaho —

The actual fort site is on the Fort Hall Indian Reservation and can't be visited, but a replica of the fort can be inspected. Inside the fort are displays covering its history. Children enjoy running around looking at the wagons and tipi inside the fort. The replica is located at Ross Park and Zoo south of the city of Pocatello, off I-15.

Three Island Crossing, Idaho —

This was a major ford of the Snake River. There is presently a state park and campground located on the north bank where the emigrants halted. There is a display in the visitor's center, a few buffalo near the campground and a beach for swimming. Thus the modern traveler is able to swim out into the Snake, close his eyes, and imagine fording the Snake as the emigrants did. The park is located just south of Glenns Ferry off I-80.

Fort Boise, Idaho —

Today the approximate location of old Fort Boise is marked only by a monument near the banks of the Snake near the ford. However, a reconstruction of the fort is underway and can be found in a small park and picnic area in Parma. When completed it will probably be filled with displays from the 1834–1855 period. It is located at the eastern edge of Parma on U.S. 20/26.

Farewell Bend, Oregon —

Here the emigrants left the Snake River. Today at the bend is a fine state park and fine Oregon Trail display. Picnicking and swimming are also allowed. Farewell Bend is located four miles south of Huntington on U.S. 30, off I-80.

Whitman Mission, Washington —

This was a major stopping place on the Trail during its early years. Today it is a National Historic Site and has a fine interpretive display and visitor center. The sites of the buildings, burned after the massacre are outlined; and the millpond, orchard, irrigation ditch, and part of the Oregon Trail have been restored. The museum deals with the mission's role and the Oregon Trail period. It is located about seven miles west of Walla Walla off U.S. 12.

The Dalles, Oregon —

Here are a number of historic sites. This is where part of the land portion ended for many people — the mouth of Chenoweth Creek. The wagons were replaced by rafts. The Methodist Mission was here, but no longer stands. Fort Dalles was here; today, only the Surgeons Quarters remains as a museum. The original courthouse still stands and is open. From the Dalles, the Barlow Road started to Oregon City. The modern Oregon traveler can choose between the Columbia River route or the land route along the Barlow Road to Oregon City.

Fort Vancouver, Washington —

This is where many of the emigrants stopped after coming down the Columbia by raft, before heading up the Willamette Valley. Today the National Park Service has reconstructed some of the buildings and the stockade itself after years of archeological work. The museum is excellent and covers the entire period from the fur trade to the settlement era. The visitor center also has a film presentation. It is located off I-5 at Mill Plain Boulevard.

Oregon City, Oregon —

This is it — the end of the trail. From here, the emigrants spread out through the Willamette Valley. The End-of-the Trail Monument, Willamette Falls, and the McLoughlin House are located here. The McLoughlin House is open and deals with his role in the Hudson's Bay Company and Oregon's development. A new "End of the Oregon Trail" Interpretive Center is now open and worth a visit.

The number of highway rest area displays and monuments are too numerous to mention and include. Many have fine displays, while others do not. Oregon's are probably the best, but all are important to the Oregon Trail's history. Many towns located along the trail also have their own museums, which may be of interest for those who have the time.

Additional Readings

NUMEROUS BOOKS have been written about the Oregon Trail since it began. However, most of them are not available in bookstores, nor are they in many public libraries. Yet, there are recent publications and reprints that are excellent. Some of these will be described briefly.

Three books are a *must* for any traveler interested in following the Oregon Trail today. Two of these books are written by Gregory M. Franzwa. His first, *The Oregon Trail Revisited,* follows the main route of the trail from Independence, Missouri, to Oregon City. It takes the modern traveler turn by turn and mile by mile along the journey. It includes locations of historical sites and comments by early emigrants as they passed through. It is outstanding and you need only to follow his directions. The book includes both a leisurely trip and a speed trip which may be used, depending upon the time available to the traveler. In some areas the trail is not accessible by modern roads or family automobile, and these places are identified.

His second book which supplements the above-mentioned book is *Maps of the Oregon Trail.* Here can be found the maps that will take the modern traveler to the Willamette and Oregon City. Oh, how the early emigrants would have loved this book! Included is not only the primary route, but also the maps showing the various major cutoffs and alternate routes which were not discussed in his first book. The maps show all the highways and other roadways with the Oregon Trail superimposed on them as a thin bright red line. Most of the maps are based on a scale of one-half inch to a mile, and they are easy to follow for even a beginning map reader. Included on the maps are the locations of many historical sites.

The third book complements both of the books mentioned already. It is Aubrey Haines' *Historic Sites Along the Oregon Trail*. He notes three hundred ninety-four sites related to Oregon Trail travel, and includes a general description of each along with its specific location and comments by historians and emigrants about each one. These sites may be found in the book of maps by Gregory Franzwa.

For the person more interested in reading about the trail and its history in depth, other books may also be found. Two fairly recent works by eminent historians are Merrill Mattes' *The Great Platte River Road* and the late John Unruh's *The Plains Across*.

Merrill Mattes' book focuses its attention on the first third of the route of the Oregon Trail and uses reference from the 1840s through the 1860s. The book includes sections on all the major "jumping off" places and their feeder routes, from Independence to the Council Bluffs area, to the junction of these feeders near Fort Kearny and then along the Platte River to Fort Laramie. Over seven hundred journals were examined and reference is made to many of them as the reader journeys westward along the trail. It is full of details about everything that concerned the emigrants, and is very easy to read.

John Unruh's *The Plains Across* is another excellent book. It focuses on the twenty year period from 1840 until 1860. Its approach is different in that it doesn't follow the trail across from its "jumping off" places, but rather, examines the interrelationship of the forces shaping the Oregon Trail experience and the changes wrought in it by time. Examined are such forces as public opinion, emigrant motivations, relations with Indians, federal government, business enterprises along the trail, and the Mormons. The emphasis is not just on each independent of the other, but as factors that impacted upon each other. As in the other books, it is full of details on such items as the price of flour at different times and at different trading posts. Emigrants' comments are widely used throughout. Both books will enable the modern traveler to understand the trek west much more clearly. Three earlier works are valuable: Bernard DeVoto's *The Year of Decision, 1846,* (1946); Jay Monaghan's *The Overland Trail* (1947); and David Lavender's *Westward Vision: The Story of the Oregon Trail* (1963).

In addition to this scholarly approach to the Oregon Trail, another view of the trail may be obtained from other books. Francis Parkman traveled from St. Louis to Fort Laramie along much of the Oregon Trail, spent some time with the Indians in the Rocky Mountains, and then returned. His accounting of his 1846 journey was first published in 1849 as *The Oregon Trail.* While it is not a journal of an emigrant, it is the firsthand experience of a traveler which is considered a classic. It is full of details about his daily experiences and his life with the Indians. Thus, the reader is able to develop a feeling of what the West was really like.

Some reprints of journals are available. Heinrich Lienhard's *From St. Louis to Sutter's Fort, 1846,* takes one half way to Oregon following the trail to Fort Bridger, and then heads to California. Thomas Farnham's *Travels in the Great Western Prairies, 1839* explains his experiences as he traveled in the Rockies and Oregon Territory. Only a few of the Oregon emigrant's journals have been printed in book form. However, many have been printed in the journals of the state historical societies. Most journals are fairly short, reprints are not very expensive, and they will provide the modern traveler with a taste of the trail. One of the longer and better ones available from the Oregon Historical Society is "From Ithaca to Clatsop Plains, Journal of Rebecca Ketcham, 1853." Rebecca started out in Westport, and by reading, you can follow her along. The journal includes a wealth of material about the sights along the trail, but perhaps more important, it allows one to get to know Rebecca's feelings and thoughts as both the joys and rigors of the trail have their impact upon her. Osborne Cross's *The March of the Mounted Riflemen* covers the length of the trail in 1849 and is very good.

There are many more books presently available or in the libraries about the emigrants and gold seekers to California, such as Bruff's *Gold Rush: Journals, Drawings, and Other Papers,* and McKinstry's *Gold Rush Overland Diary of Byron N. Mckinstry 1850–1852.* As with Lienhard's, mentioned earlier these cover only part of the trail. They extend farther, to Fort Hall. However, they are very good. Other books will also be released soon on the experiences of women on the trail, and a series of overland diaries by period is to be published.

All the books mentioned will provide the modern traveler with a variety of information enabling one to locate, travel, and feel the Oregon Trail. For those wishing to delve further, the bibliographies of Franzwa's, Mattes', Haines', and Unruh's books are extensive. Also, as one travels along trail, most of the visitor centers at the various major historical sites have small books and pamphlets which should be examined.

Happy Reading! Happy Traveling!

Part V
Bibliography

Bibliography

BOOKS, BOOKLETS AND ARTICLES:

Driggs, Howard R. *Westward America*. New York: J. B. Lippencott, 1942.

Franzwa, Gregory. *Maps of the Oregon Trail*. Gerald, Mo.: Patrice Press, 1982.

———. *The Oregon Trail Revisited*. St. Louis: Patrice Press, 1972.

Ghent, W. J. *The Road to Oregon, A Chronical of the Great Emigrant Trail*. New York: Tudor, 1934.

Gilbert, William, and others. *The Trail Blazers*. New York: Time/Life Books, 1973.

Haines, Aubrey, *Historic Sites Along the Oregon Trail*. Gerald, Mo.: Patrice Press, 1981.

Harris, Earl R. *Courthouse and Jail Rocks*. Nebraska State Historical Society, 1962.

Horn, Huston, *The Pioneers*. New York: Time/Life Books, 1974

Jackson, William Henry. *Time Exposure*. New York: G. P. Putnam's Sons, 1940.

Mattes, Merrill J. *The Great Platte River Road*. Nebraska Historical Society, 1969.

———. *Chimney Rock Nebraska*, Nebraska State Historical Society, 1978.

———. *Scotts Bluff*, Washington, D.C.: National Park Service, 1976.

Josephy, Jr., Alvin. "A Most Satisfactory Council." *American Heritage*, Vol. 16, Oct. 1965, pp. 27–31 ff.

——— ."First 'Dude Ranch' Trip to the Untamed West," *American Heritage*, Vol. 7, Feb. 1956.

Martin, Gene and Mary. *Trail Dust*. Manitou Springs, Colo.: Martin Associates, 1972.

Ross, Marvin C. *The West of Alfred Jacob Miller*. Norman: University of Oklahoma Press, 1968.

Smith, William E. "The Oregon Trail Through Pottawatomie County," *Collection of the Kansas State Historical Society*, Vol. 17, 1926-28.

Stegner, Wallace, and others. "The Oregon Trail . . . Road To Destiny." *Trails West*. Washington, D.C.: *National Geographic Society*, 1979.

Unruh, John. *The Plains Across: The Overland Emigrants and the Trans-Mississippi West, 1840-60*. Chicago: University of Illinois Press, 1979.

Wagner, Henry R. *The Plains and the Rockies: A Bibliography of Original Narratives of Travel and Adventure 1800-1865*. Columbus: Long's College Book Co., 1953.

Young, F. "The Oregon Trail." *Oregon Historical Quarterly*, Vol. 1, Dec. 1900: pp. 339–370.

————. *Barlow Road*. Wasco and Clackamas County Historical Society, Portland: Hollingsworth Co., 1976.

————. *Oregon Trail, National Historic Trail, Comprehensive Management and Use Plan, Appendix II and III*. National Park Service, August 1981.

JOURNALS AND GUIDEBOOKS:

Adams, Cecelia E. M. "Crossing the Plains in 1852." *Transactions, O.P.A.* 1904: 288–329.

Allen, A. *Ten Years in Oregon — Travels and Adventure in Oregon*. Ithaca: Mack, Andrew Co., 1848.

Allyn, Henry. "Journal of Henry Allyn, 1853." *Transactions, O.P.A.* 1921: 372–435.

Applegate, Jesse. "A Day with the Cow Column in 1843." *Oregon Historical Quarterly*, I Dec. 1900: 371–383.

Ball, John. "Across the Continent Seventy Years Ago." *Oregon Historical Quarterly*, III 1902: 82–107.

Belshaw, Maria P. "Diary of Marcia Parsons Belshaw, 1853." Ed., J. W. Ellison, *Oregon Historical Quarterly*, XXXIII Dec. 1932: 318–33.

Burnett, Peter H., "Recollections and Opinions of an Old Pioneer." *Oregon Historical Quarterly*, V 1904: 64–99.

Bruff, J. Goldsborough. *Gold Rush: Journals, Drawings, And Other Papers*. Ed., Georgia Willis Read and Ruth Gaines. New York: Columbia Press, 1949.

Clayton, William. *Latter-Day Saints 'Emigrants' Guide*. St. Louis: Chambers & Knapp, 1848 (Reprint: Ed., Stanley Kimball, Patrice Press, 1983).

Child, Andrew. *Overland Route to California*. Milwaukee: Daily Sentinel Steam Power Press, 1852.

Conyers, E. W. "Dairy of E. W. Conyers, A Pioneer of 1852." *Transactions, O.P.A.* 1905: 423–512.

Crawford, Medorem. "Journal of Medorem Crawford," Fairfield, Washington: Ye Galleon Press, 1967.

Crawford, P. V. "Journal of a Trip Across the Plains, 1851." *Oregon Historical Quarterly*, XXV June 1924: 136–69.

Cross, Osborne. *The March of the Mounted Riflemen*. Ed., Raymand W. Settle, Glendale, Calif.: The Arthur H. Clark Co., 1940.

Farnham, Thomas J. *Travels in the Great Western Prairies, A Wagon Train Journal*. (1843) (Reprint by Rodney R. McCallum, Monroe, Oregon)

Fremont, John Charles. *The Expeditions of J. C. Fremont*. (Ed., Donald Jackson & Mary Lee Spence.) Urbana: University of Illinois Press, 1970: Vol. I and II and maps.

Hale, Israel. "Dairy of Trip to California." *Society of California Pioneers Quarterly*, Vol. 2: 61–130.

Hastings, L. W. *The Emigrants' Guide to Oregon and California* (1845). (Reprint, Princeton: Princeton University Press, 1932.)

Hines, Celinda E. "Diary of Celinda Hines." *Transactions, O.P.A.* 1918: 69–125.

Horn, Hosea. *Horn's Overland Guide.* New York: J. H. Colton, 1852.

Johnson, Overton, and Winters, William H. *Route Across The Rocky Mountains.* Lafayette, Ind. 1846. (Reprint Ann Arbor: University of Michigan. Microfilm, Inc. 1966)

Ketcham, Rebecca. "From Ithaca to Clatsop Plains." *Oregon Historical Quarterly,* LXII Sept. 1961: 237–87 and Dec. 1961: 337–402.

Kerns, John T. "Journal of Crossing the Plains to Oregon in 1852," *Transactions, O.P.A.* 1914: 148–93.

Lienhard, Heinrich. *From St. Louis to Sutters Fort, 1846.* (Ed., Gudde, Erwin, & Elizabeth) Norman: University of Oklahoma Press, 1961.

Marcy, Randolph B. *The Prairie Traveler, A Handbook for Overland Expeditions.* New York: Harper & Bros., 1859.

Minto, John, "Reminiscenes of Honorable John Minto, Pioneer of 1844," *Oregon Historical Quarterly,* II June 1901: 119–67.

Munger, Aschel, "Diary of Aschel Munger and Wife," *Oregon Historical Quarterly,* VIII Dec. 1907: 387–415.

Nesmith, James W. "Diary of the Emigration of 1843," *Oregon Historical Quarterly,* VII Dec. 1906: 329–59.

Newby, William T. "Diary of the Emigration of 1843," *Oregon Historical Quarterly,* XL Sept. 1939: 219–42.

Palmer, Joel. *Journal of Travels Over the Rocky Mountains (1845-46).* Cincinnati: J. A. & U. P. James, 1847. (Reprint Ann Arbor: University of Michigan. Microfilm, Inc. 1966)

Parkman, Francis. *The Oregon Trail.* New York: New American Library, 1950. (reprint)

Reading, P. B. "Journal of Pierson Barton Reading." *Society of California Pioneers, Quarterly.* Vol. 6, 148–198.

Stansbury, Howard. *An Expedition to the Valley of the Great Salt Lake.* (Reprint Ann Arbor: University of Michigan. Microfilm, Inc. 1966)

Steward, Agnes. "The Journey to Oregon: A Pioneer Girl's Diary," ed., C. W. Churchill, *Oregon Historical Quarterly,* XXIX March 1928, 77–98.

Snyder, Jacob R. "The Diary of Jacob R. Snyder," *Society of California Pioneers, Quarterly,* Vol. 8, 1931, 224–60.

Ware, Joseph. *The Emigrant's Guide to California.* St. Louis: J. Halsall, 1849.

Wilkins, James F. *An Artist on the Overland Trail: The 1849 Diary and Sketches of James F. Wilkins* (Ed., John F. McDermott), San Marino: The Huntington Library, 1968.

Williams, Velina A. "Diary of a Trip Across the Plains in 1853," *Transactions, O.P.A.* 1919, 178–226.

PAMPHLETS:

"Chimney Rock," National Park Service, Washington, D.C., 1974.

"Fort Bridger," Wyoming Recreation Department, State Archives & Historical Department.

"Fort Dalles Museum," The Dalles Museum Commission.

"Fort Kearny," Nebraska State Historical Society. Ed. Leaflet No. 7.

"Fort Laramie," National Park Service, Washington, D.C.

"Fort Vancouver," National Park Service, Washington, D.C.

"Hollenberg Pony Express Station," Kansas State Historical Society.

"Old Fort Hall," City of Pocatello, Parks and Recreation Department.

"The Oregon Trail," National Park Service, Washington, D.C. 1982.

"The Oregon Trail," Nebraska Game and Parks Commission.

"Oregon Trail," Oregon State Highway Division.

"Route of the Oregon Trail in Idaho," Idaho Historical Society Bicentennial Commission and the Idaho Transportation Department, 1974.

"Scotts Bluff," National Park Service, Washington, D.C., 1978.

"Shawnee Methodist Mission and Indian Manual Labor School," Kansas State Historical Society.

"Three Island Crossing," Idaho Department of Parks and Recreation.

"Whitman Mission," National Park Service, Washington, D.C., 1978 and 1974.

Part VI
Index

Index